First International Workshop on Spatial Language Understanding (SpLU-2018)

New Orleans, Louisiana, USA
6 June 2018

ISBN: 978-1-5108-6363-7

Printed from e-media with permission by:

Curran Associates, Inc.
57 Morehouse Lane
Red Hook, NY 12571

Some format issues inherent in the e-media version may also appear in this print version.

Copyright© (2018) by the Association for Computational Linguistics
All rights reserved.

Printed by Curran Associates, Inc. (2018)

For permission requests, please contact the Association for Computational Linguistics
at the address below.

Association for Computational Linguistics
209 N. Eighth Street
Stroudsburg, Pennsylvania 18360

Phone: 1-570-476-8006
Fax: 1-570-476-0860

acl@aclweb.org

Additional copies of this publication are available from:

Curran Associates, Inc.
57 Morehouse Lane
Red Hook, NY 12571 USA
Phone: 845-758-0400
Fax: 845-758-2633
Email: curran@proceedings.com
Web: www.proceedings.com

NAACL HLT 2018

**Spatial Language Understanding
(SpLU-2018)**

Proceedings of the First International Workshop

June 6, 2018
New Orleans, Louisiana

©2018 The Association for Computational Linguistics

Introduction

The SpLU-2018 is the first international workshop on spatial language understanding. One of the essential functions of natural language is to express spatial relationships between objects. Linguistic constructs can encode highly complex, relational structures of objects, spatial relations between them, and patterns of motion through space relative to some reference point. Spatial language understanding is useful in many areas of research endeavors relating to and/or making use of human language, including robotics, navigation, geographic information systems, traffic management, natural language understanding and translation, and query answering systems. Compared to other semantically specialized linguistic tasks, standardizing tasks related to spatial language seems to be more challenging as it is harder to obtain an agreeable set of concepts and relationships and a formal spatial meaning representation that is domain independent, as an example this could be compared to temporal relations. This has made research results on spatial language learning and reasoning diverse, task-specific and, to some extent, not comparable. While formal meaning representation is a general issue for language understanding, formalizing spatial concepts and building formal reasoning models based on those constitute challenging research problems with a wealth of prior foundational research that can be exploited and linked to language understanding. Existing qualitative and quantitative representation and reasoning models can be used for investigation of interoperability of machine learning and reasoning over spatial semantics. Research endeavors in this area could provide insights into many challenges of language understanding in general. Spatial semantics is also very well-connected and relevant to visualization of natural language, central to dealing with configurations in the physical world and motivating a combination of vision and language for richer spatial understanding. This workshop aims to highlight some of the above aspects of computational spatial language understanding including the following four areas: 1)Spatial Language Meaning Representation (Continuous, Symbolic) 2) Spatial Language Learning 3) Spatial Language Reasoning 4) Combining Vision and Language for Spatial Understanding.

This year we accepted eight papers covering various aspects of spatial language understanding, including semantic analysis of the usage of spatial language, metaphorical usage of spatial language, how spatial concepts are formalized in FrameNet, understanding spatial language for environments like block world and spatial description generation in a dialogue system given a multi-modal setting, generation of large-scale annotated corpora with spatial concepts and primitives, machine learning models for spatial information extraction and resolving anaphora in spatial relations. We have invited two internationally recognized speakers and organized a panel including the senior members of our organizing and program committee to discuss the key-points and issues raised during the workshop.

Finally, we would like to thank all programming committee members, speakers, and authors. We are looking forward to seeing you in New Orleans.

Organizers:

Parisa Kordjamshidi, Tulane University, Florida Institute for Human and Machine Cognition
Archna Bhatia, Florida Institute for Human and Machine Cognition
James Pustejovsky, Brandeis University
Marie-Francine Moens, KU Leuven

Program Committee:

John A. Bateman, Universität Bremen
Anthony G. Cohn, University of Leeds
Steven Bethard, The University of Arizona
Raffaella Bernardi, University of Trento
Mehul Bhatt, Örebro University, Universität Bremen
Yonatan Bisk, University of Washington
Johan Bos, University of Groningen
Joyce Chai, Michigan State University
Angel Xuan Chang, Stanford University
Guillem Collell, KU Leuven
Zoe Falomir, Universität Bremen
Julia Hockenmaier, University of Illinois at Urbana-Champaign
Kirk Roberts, UT Health Science Center at Houston
Manolis Savva, Princeton University
Martijn van Otterlo, Vrije Universiteit Amsterdam
Bonnie Dorr, Florida Institute for Human and Machine Cognition
Bruno Martins, University of Lisbon
Mari Broman Olsen, Microsoft
Clare Voss, ARL
Umar Manzoor, Tulane University

Invited Speaker:

Anthony G. Cohn, University of Leeds
James F. Allen, Florida Institute for Human and Machine Cognition, University of Rochester

Panelists:

James Pustejovsky, Brandeis University
Marie-Francine Moens, KU Leuven
James F. Allen, Florida Institute for Human and Machine Cognition, University of Rochester
Bonnie Dorr, Florida Institute for Human and Machine Cognition
Anthony G. Cohn, University of Leeds

Table of Contents

Workshop Program

June 6, 2018

Session 1

09:00–09:10   *Opening remarks*
Parisa Kordjamshidi

09:10–10:10   *Keynote talk: Natural Language Acquisition and Grounding for Embodied Robotic Systems*
Anthony G. Cohn

10:10–10:30   *Exploring the Functional and Geometric Bias of Spatial Relations Using Neural Language Models*
Simon Dobnik, Mehdi Ghanimifard and John Kelleher

10:30–11:00   Coffee Break

Session 2

11:00–11:20   *Building and Learning Structures in a Situated Blocks World Through Deep Language Understanding*
Ian Perera, James Allen, Choh Man Teng and Lucian Galescu

11:20–11:40   *Computational Models for Spatial Prepositions*
Georgiy Platonov and Lenhart Schubert

11:40–12:00   *Lexical Conceptual Structure of Literal and Metaphorical Spatial Language: A Case Study of "Push"*
Bonnie Dorr and Mari Olsen

12:00–12:20   *Representing Spatial Relations in FrameNet*
Miriam R L Petruck and Michael J Ellsworth

12:20–02:10   **Lunch Break**

Session 3

02:10–03:10   *Keynote talk: Understanding Spatial Expressions*
James F. Allen

03:10–03:30   *Points, Paths, and Playscapes: Large-scale Spatial Language Understanding Tasks Set in the Real World*
Jason Baldridge, Tania Bedrax-Weiss, Daphne Luong, Srini Narayanan, Bo Pang, Fernando Pereira, Radu Soricut, Michael Tseng and Yuan Zhang

03:30–04:00   **Coffee Break**

Session 4

04:00–04:20   *Anaphora Resolution for Improving Spatial Relation Extraction from Text*
Umar Manzoor and Parisa Kordjamshidi

04:20–04:40   *The Case for Systematically Derived Spatial Language Usage*
Bonnie Dorr and Clare Voss

04:40–05:30   *Panel*
James Pustejovsky, Marie-Francine Moens, James F. Allen, Bonnie Dorr, Anthony G. Cohn

Exploring the Functional and Geometric Bias of Spatial Relations Using Neural Language Models

Simon Dobnik[*]   **Mehdi Ghanimifard**[*]   **John D. Kelleher**[†]
[*]CLASP and FLOV, University of Gothenburg, Sweden
[†]Dublin Institute of Technology, Ireland
[*]{simon.dobnik,mehdi.ghanimifard}@gu.se [†]john.d.kelleher@dit.ie

Abstract

The challenge for computational models of spatial descriptions for situated dialogue systems is the integration of information from different modalities. The semantics of spatial descriptions are grounded in at least two sources of information: (i) a geometric representation of space and (ii) the functional interaction of related objects that. We train several neural language models on descriptions of scenes from a dataset of image captions and examine whether the functional or geometric bias of spatial descriptions reported in the literature is reflected in the estimated perplexity of these models. The results of these experiments have implications for the creation of models of spatial lexical semantics for human-robot dialogue systems. Furthermore, they also provide an insight into the kinds of the semantic knowledge captured by neural language models trained on spatial descriptions, which has implications for image captioning systems.

1 Introduction

Spatial language understanding is fundamental requirement for human-robot interaction through dialogue. A natural task for a human to request a robot to fulfil is to retrieve or replace an object for them. Consequently, a particularly frequent form of spatial description within human-robot interaction is a *locative expression*. A locative expression is a noun phrase that describes the location of one object (the *target object*) relative to another object (the *landmark*). The relative location of the target object is specified through a prepositional phrase:

Bring me *the big red book* on *the table*.

Target   *Landmark*
Prepositional Phrase
Locative Expression

In order to understand these forms of spatial descriptions a robot must be equipped with computational models of the spatial semantics of prepositions that enable them to ground the semantics of the locative expression relative to the context of the situated dialogue.

A natural approach to developing these computational models is to define them in terms of scene *geometry*. And, indeed, there is a tradition of research that follows this path, see for example (Logan and Sadler, 1996; Kelleher and Costello, 2005, 2009). However, there is also a body of experimental and computational research that has highlighted that the semantics of spatial descriptions are dependent on several sources of information beyond scene geometry, including *functional semantics* (which encompasses a range of factors such as world knowledge about the typical interactions between objects, and object affordances) (Coventry and Garrod, 2004). We can illustrate this distinction between geometric and functionally defined semantics using a number of examples. To illustrate a geometric semantics: assuming a spatial meaning, anything can be described as *to left of* anything else so long the spatial configuration of the two objects is geometrically correct. However, as (Coventry et al., 2001) has shown the spatial description *the umbrella is over the man* is sensitive to the protective affordances of the umbrella to stop rain, and is appropriate in contexts where, the umbrella is not in a geometrically prototypical position above the man, so long as the umbrella is protecting the man from the rain.

A further complication with regard to modelling the semantics of spatial descriptions is that experimental results indicate that the contribution of geometrical and functional factors is not the same for every spatial relation (Garrod et al., 1999; Coventry et al., 2001). This experimental work shows that there is an interplay between function and ge-

1

Proceedings of the First International Workshop on Spatial Language Understanding (SpLU-2018), pages 1–11
New Orleans, Louisiana, June 6, 2018. ©2018 Association for Computational Linguistics

ometry in the definition of spatial semantics and therefore the spatial meaning of given spatial relation is neither fully functional nor fully geometric. Rather, spatial terms can be ordered on a spectrum based on the sensitivity of their semantics to geometric or functional factors.

Given the distinction between geometric and functional factors in shaping spatial semantics, a useful analysis that would inform the design and creation of computational models of spatial semantics is *to identify the particular semantic bias (geometric/functional) that each spatial term evinces.* However, such an analysis is difficult. Native speakers do not have strong intuitions about the bias of prepositions and such bias had to be established experimentally (Coventry et al., 2001; Garrod et al., 1999) or through linguistic analysis (Herskovits, 1986, p.55).[1] Reviewing the literature on this experimental and analytic work reveals that prepositions such as *in*, *on*, *at*, *over*, *under* have been identified as being functionally biased, whereas *above*, *below*, *left of* and *right of* are geometrically biased. Other spatial relations may be somewhere in between. In this paper we will use these relations as ground-truth pointers against which our methods will be evaluated. If the method is successful, then we are able to make predictions about those relations that have not been verified for their bias experimentally. Knowing the bias of a spatial relation is useful both theoretically and practically. Theoretically, it informs us about the complexity of grounded semantics of spatial relations. In particular, it engages with the "what" and "where" debate where it has been argued that spatial relations are not only spatial (i.e. geometric) (Landau and Jackendoff, 1993; Coventry and Garrod, 2004; Landau, 2016). Practically, the procedure to estimate the bias is useful for natural language generation systems, for example in situated robotic applications that cannot be trained end-to-end. Given that a particular pair of objects can be described geometrically with several spatial relations, the knowledge of functional bias may be used as a filter, prioritising those relations that are more likely for a particular pair of objects, thereby incorporat-

___
[1] The discussion of Herskovits focuses on interaction of objects conceptualised as geometric shapes, for example *on:* contiguity with line or surface. The fact that the interacting objects can be conceptualised as different geometric shapes points and therefore related by a particular prepositions points to their functional nature as discussed here.

ing functional knowledge. This approach to generation of spatial descriptions is therefore similar to the approach that introduces a cognitive load based hierarchy of spatial relations (Kelleher and Kruijff, 2006) or a classification-based approach that combines geometric (related to the bounding box), textual (word2vec embeddings) and visual features (final layer of a convolutional network) (Ramisa et al., 2015). The functional geometric bias of spatial relations could also be used to inform semantic parsing, for example in prepositional phrase attachment resolution (Christie et al., 2016; Delecraz et al., 2017).

Previous work has investigated metrics of the semantic bias of spatial prepositions, see (Dobnik and Kelleher, 2013, 2014). (Dobnik and Kelleher, 2013) uses (i) normalised entropy of target-landmark pairs to estimate variation of targets and landmarks per relation and (ii) log likelihood ratio to predict the strength of association of target-landmark pairs with a spatial relation and presents ranked lists of relations by the degree of argument variation or strength of the association respectively. The approach hypothesises that functionally biased relations are more selective in the kind of targets and landmarks they co-occur with. The reasoning behind this is that geometrically it is possible to relate a wider range of objects than in the case where additional functional constrains between objects are also applied. (Dobnik and Kelleher, 2014) generalises over landmarks and targets in WordNet hierarchy and estimates the generality of the types of landmark. Again, the work hypothesises that functional relations are more restricted in their choice of target and landmark objects and therefore are generally more specific in terms of the WordNet hierarchy. Both papers present results compatible with the hypotheses where the functional or geometric nature of prepositions is predicted in line with the experimental studies (Garrod et al., 1999; Coventry et al., 2001).

Sensitive to the fact that relations such as *in* and *on* not only have spatial usage but also usages that may be considered metaphoric (Steen et al., 2010), both (Dobnik and Kelleher, 2013) and (Dobnik and Kelleher, 2014) were based on an analysis of a corpus of image captions. The idea being that descriptions of images are more likely to contain spatial descriptions grounded in the image. For similar reasons, we also employ a corpus of image descriptions (larger than in the previous work).

This paper adopts a similar research hypothesis to (Dobnik and Kelleher, 2014, 2013), namely that: it is possible to distinguish between functionally biased and geometrically biased spatial relations by examining the diversity of the contexts in which they occur. Defining the concept of context in terms of the *target* and *landmark* object pairs that a relation occurs within, the rationale of this hypothesis is that: geometrically biased relations are more likely to be observed in a more diverse set of contexts, compared to functionally biased relations, because the use of a geometrically biased relation only presupposes the appropriate geometric configuration whereas the use of a functionally biased relation is also constrained by object affordances or typical interactions.

However, the work presented in this paper provides a more general analytical technique based on a neural language model (Bengio et al., 2003; Mikolov et al., 2010) which is applied to a larger dataset of spatial descriptions. We use neural language models as the basic tool for our analysis because they are already commonly used to learn the syntax and semantics of words in an unsupervised way. The contribution of this paper in relation to (i) the previous analyses of geometric and functional aspects of spatial relations is that it examines whether similar predictions can be made using these more general tools of representing meaning of words and phrases; the contribution to (ii) deep learning of language and vision is that it examines to what extent highly specific world-knowledge can be extracted from a neural language model. The paper proceeds as follows: in Section 2 we describe the datasets and their processing, in Section 3 we describe the basics behind language models and the notion of perplexity, in Section 4 and 5 we present and discuss our results. We conclude in Section 6.

The code that was used to produce the datasets and results discussed in this paper can be found at: `https://github.com/GU-CLASP/functional-geometric-lm`.

2   Datasets

The Amsterdam Metaphor Corpus (Steen et al., 2010) which is based on a subsection of a BNC reveals that the spatial sense of prepositions are very rare in genres such as news, fiction and academic texts. For example, *below* only has two instances that are not labelled as a metaphor and more than 60% of fragments with *in*, *on*, and *over* are not used in their spatial sense. For this reason Dobnik and Kelleher (2013) use two image description corpora (IAPR TC-12 (Grubinger et al., 2006) and Flickr8k (Rashtchian et al., 2010)) where spatial uses of prepositions are common. They apply a dependency parser and a set of post-processing rules to extract spatial relations, target and landmark object triplets. The size of this extracted dataset is 96,749 instances and is relatively small for training a neural language model. (Kordjamshidi et al., 2017) released CLEF 2017 multimodal spatial role labelling dataset (mSpRL) which is a human annotated subset of the IAPR TC-12 Benchmark corpus for spatial relations, targets and landmarks (Kordjamshidi et al., 2011) containing 613 text files and 1,213 sentences. While this dataset could not be used to train a language model directly, a spatial role labelling classifier could be trained on it to identify spatial relations and arguments which would then be used to produce a bootstrapped dataset for training a neural language model.

Recently, Visual Genome (Krishna et al., 2017) has been released which is a crowd-source annotated corpus of 108K images which also includes annotations of *relationships* between (previously annotated) bounding boxes. Relationships are predicates that relate objects which include spatial relations (2404639, "cup on table"), verbs (2367163, "girl holding on to bear") as well as combinations of verbs and spatial relations (2317920, "woman standing on snow") and others. We use this dataset in the work reported here. Its advantage is that it contains a large number of annotated relationships but the disadvantage is that these are collected in a crowd-sourced setting and are therefore sometimes noisy but we assume these are still of better quality than those from a bootstrapped machine annotated dataset.

To extract spatial relations from the annotated relationships, we created a dictionary of their syntactic forms based on the lists of English spatial relations in Landau (1996) and Herskovits (1986). For the training data we preserve all items annotated as relationships as single tokens ("jumping_over") and we simplify some of the composite spatial relations based on our dictionary, e.g. "left of" and "to the left of" become "left" to increase the frequency of instances. This choice could have affected our results if done without careful consideration. While compound variants of spatial relations have slightly different meanings, we only collapsed those relations for which we assumed this would not affect their geometric or functional bias. Furthermore, Dobnik and Kelleher (2013) show that compound relations cluster with their non-compound variants using normalised entropy of target-landmark pairs as a metric. Finally, some variation was due to the shorthand notation used by the annotators, e.g. "to left of". The reason behind keeping all relation(ships) in the training set is to train the language model on as many targets and landmarks as possible and to learn paradigmatic relations between them. We normalise all words to lowercase and remove the duplicate descriptions per image (created by different annotators). We also check for and remove instances where a spatial relation is used as an object, e.g. "chair on left". We remove instances where one of the words has fewer than 100 occurrences in the whole dataset which reduces the dataset size by 10%. We add start and end tokens to the triplets ($\langle s \rangle$ *target relation landmark* $\langle /s \rangle$) as required for training and testing a language model. The dataset is shuffled and split into 10 folds that are later used in cross-validation. In the evaluation, we take 20 samples per spatial relation from the held out data of those relations that are members of the dictionary created previously. This way the average perplexity is always calculated on the same number of samples per each relation.[2]

3 Language model and perplexity

3.1 Language model

Probabilistic language models capture the sequential properties of language or paradigmatic relations between sequences of words. Using the chain rules of probabilities they estimate the likelihood of a sequence of words:

$$P(w_{1:T}) = \sum_{t=1}^{T} P(w_{t+1}|w_{1:t}) \tag{1}$$

Neural language models estimate probabilities by optimising parameters of a function represented in a neural architecture (Bengio et al., 2003):

$$\hat{P}(w_{t+1}|w_{1:t} = v_{k_{1:t}}) = f(v_{t-1}; \Theta) = \hat{y}_t \tag{2}$$

where Θ represents parameters of the model, f being the composition of functions within the neural network architecture, and $v_{k_{1:t}}$ the words up to time t in the sequence. The output of the function is $\hat{y}_t \in R^n$, a vector of probabilities, with each dimension representing the probability of a word in the vocabulary. The loss of a recurrent language model is the average surprisal for each batch of data (Graves et al., 2013; Mikolov et al., 2010):

$$loss(S) = -\sum_{s \in S} \sum_{t=0}^{|s|} \frac{\log(\hat{y}_t(v_{k_{t+1}}))}{|S| \times |s|} \tag{3}$$

Note that our architecture is deliberately simple as we apply it in an experimental setting with constrained descriptions[3]. We use a Keras implementation (Chollet et al., 2015), and fit the model parameters with Adam (Kingma and Ba, 2014) with a batch size of 32 and iterations of 20 epochs. On each iteration the language model is optimised on the loss which is related to perplexity as described in the following section.

3.2 Perplexity

Instead of calculating the averages of likelihoods from Equation 1, which might get very low on long sequences of text, we use perplexity which is an exponential measure for average negative log likelihoods of the model. This solves the representation problem with floating points and large samples of data.

$$Perplexity(S, P) = 2^{E_S[-log_2(P(w_{1:T}))]} \tag{4}$$

where $w_{1:T}$ is an instance in a sample collection S. Perplexity is often used for evaluating language models on test sets. Since language models are optimised for low perplexities[4], the perplexity of a trained model can be used as a measure of fit of the model with the samples.

4 Varying targets and landmarks

4.1 Hypotheses

As a language model encodes semantic relations between words in a sequence we therefore expect that the distinction between functional and geometric spatial relations will also be captured by

---

[2]The reason we use 20 sample is that this is also the size of the 10% test folds in the down-sampled dataset described later. In selecting 20 items for the test-set we also ensure that it contains the vocabulary in the down-sampled training folds.

[3]For more details on the architecture see Section A.1 in the supplementary material, in particular Figure 6 and Equation 5.

[4]Equation 4 is related to Equation 3 as perplexity is 2^{Loss} given a neural model as the likelihood model.

it. As functionally biased spatial relations are used in different situational contexts than geometrically biased spatial relations, we expect that a language model will capture this bias in different distributions of target and landmark objects in the forms of the perplexity of phrases. Our weak hypothesis is that the perplexity of phrases on the test set reflects the functional-geometric bias of a spatial relation (Hypothesis 1). We take the assumption that functionally-biased relations are more selective in terms of their target and landmark choice (Section 1) and consequently sequences such as <s> target relation landmark </s> with functional relations have a higher predictability in the dataset resulting in a lower perplexity in the language model (Hypothesis 2). Related to this hypothesis, there is a stronger hypothesis that target and landmark are predictable with a given functional spatial relation (Hypothesis 3).

4.2 Method

We train two language models as described in Section 3.1. For training and evaluation 10-fold cross-validation is used and average results are reported. We ensure that the evaluation sets contain no vocabulary not seen during the training. The language model 1 (LM1) is trained on unrestricted frequencies of instances. In training the language model 2 (LM2) we down-sample relations so that they are represented with equal frequencies. The dataset to train LM2 contains 200 instances of each possible relations while the evaluation set contains 20 instances for each spatial relation. Note that using this method some targeted spatial relations might disappear from the evaluation set as their frequency in the held-out data is too low. In addition to the requirement that the evaluation set contains no out-of-vocabulary items, the target and landmarks are included without restriction on their frequency, as they occur with these spatial relations.

4.3 Results

Figure 1 shows the estimated average perplexities of a subset of spatial relations, those that satisfy the sampling frequency requirement described in Section 4.2. Functionally and geometrically biased spatial relations as identified experimentally in the literature (Section 1) are represented with orange and blue bars respectively. There is a tendency that functionally biased relations lead to lower mean perplexity of phrases (Hypothesis

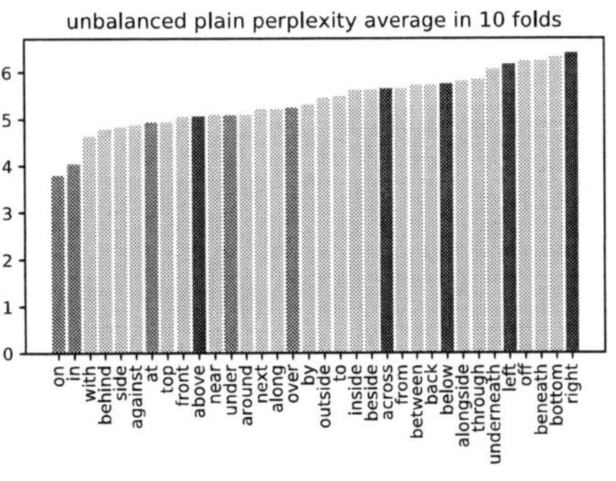

(a) test-set

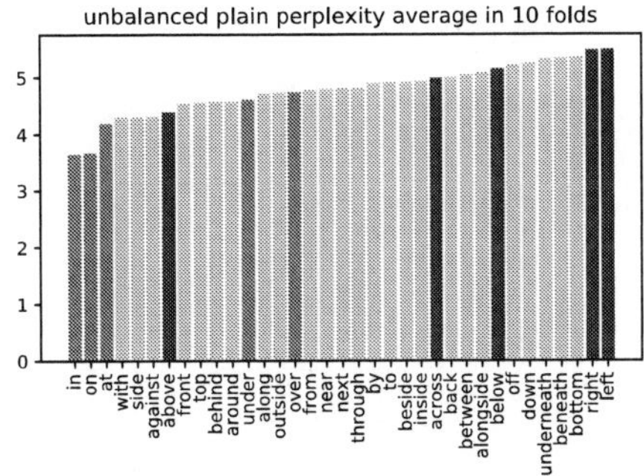

(b) training set

Figure 1: Mean perplexities of spatial descriptions of LM1 (orange: functionally biased, blue: geometrically biased relations).

2 is confirmed) and also that there is a tendency that spatial relations of a particular bias cluster together (Hypothesis 1 is also confirmed). We report results both on the training set and the test set which show the same tendencies. This means that our model generalises well on the test set and that the latter is representative.

However, in the language model the perplexities are biased by the frequency of individual words: more frequent words are more likely and therefore they are associated with lower LM perplexity. The results show high Spearman's rank correlation coefficient $\rho = 0.90$ between frequencies of spatial relation in the dataset and the perplexity of the model on the test set: on (329,529) $>$ in (108,880) $>$ under (11,631) $>$ above (8,952) $>$ over (5,714) $>$ at (4,890) $>$ below (2,290) $>$ across (1,230) $>$ left (996) $>$ right (891). For the purposes of our investigation in predictability of target-landmark pairs (Hypothesis 3) we should avoid the bias in the training set. In order to exclude the bias of frequencies of relations, we evaluate LM2 where spatial relations are presented with equal frequen-

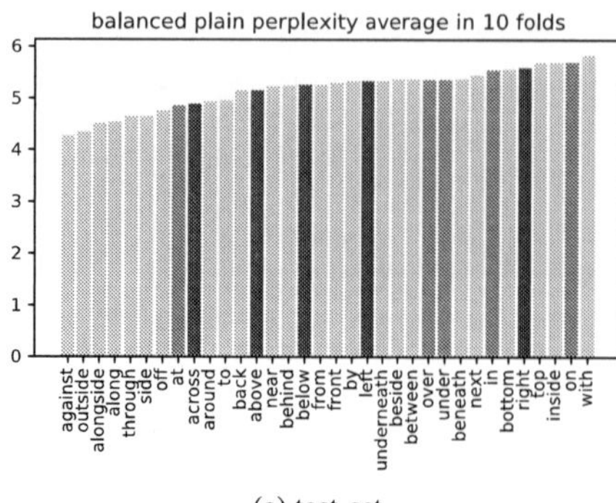

(a) test-set

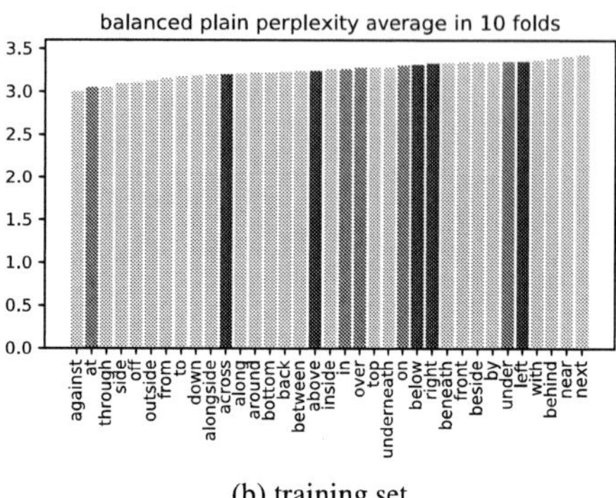

(b) training set

Figure 2: Mean perplexities of LM2 by spatial relation (orange: functionally biased, blue: geometrically biased).

cies in training. Figure 2 shows the ranking of spatial relations by the perplexities when the language model was trained with balanced frequencies. The two kinds of spatial relations are less clearly separable as the colours overlap (Hypothesis 3 is not confirmed). In comparison to Figure 1 there is an observable trend that all instances lead to lower perplexities in the training set which is the effect of down-sampling on vocabulary size. Figure 2 also shows that phrases with geometrically biased spatial relations have a higher change towards lower perplexities.

Noting that the frequency of using functionally-biased spatial relations are higher in English, this bias and our strong hypothesis for predictability of target-landmark pairs can be expressed with simple joint probabilities which we are estimating with the language model:

$$P(target, relation, landmark) =$$

$$P(relation)P(target, landmark|relation)$$

It is possible that targets and landmarks that occur with these relations are very specific to these rela-

tions but infrequent with other relations. When we remove their frequency support provided by the frequency of relations these targets and landmarks become infrequent in the dataset and therefore less probable which on overall results in higher perplexities of phrases with functionally-biased relations. Specificity of targets and landmarks can be a source of these results.

To provide (some) evidence for this assumption, Figure 3 shows the average ratios of unique types over total types of targets and landmarks in the balanced dataset over 10-folds on which LM2 was trained. There is a very clear division between functionally and geometrically biased spatial relations in terms of the uniqueness of targets, functionally-biased relations are occurring with more unique ones which contributes to higher perplexity of LM2. There is less clear distinction between the two kinds of spatial relations in terms of uniqueness of landmarks. Some functional relations such as *on* occur with fewer unique landmarks than targets (from .11 to .06), some geometric relations such as *right* occur with more unique landmarks than targets (from .07 to .11). The asymmetry between targets and landmarks is expected since the choice of landmarks in the image description task is restricted by the choice of the targets (as well as other contextual factors such as visual salience). They have to be "good landmarks" to relate the targets to. A functional relation-landmark pair is more related to the target through the landmark's affordances whereas a geometric relation-landmark pair is more related to the target through geometry. This might explain for example, why *on* has fewer, but *right* has more unique landmarks than targets. On the other hand there are also relations where the ratio of unique targets and landmarks is very similar, for example *at* (.14 and .14). Overall, it appears that if uniqueness of objects is contributing to the perplexity of the language model of phrases which functionally-biased relations (which in this balanced dataset is the case) then this is more contributed by targets rather than the landmarks.

To further explore the idea of asymmetry between targets and landmarks we re-arranged the targets and landmarks in the descriptions from the balanced dataset that LM2 was trained to <s> landmark relation target </s> and trained LM2′. The average perplexities over 10-folds of cross-validation are shown in Figure 4.

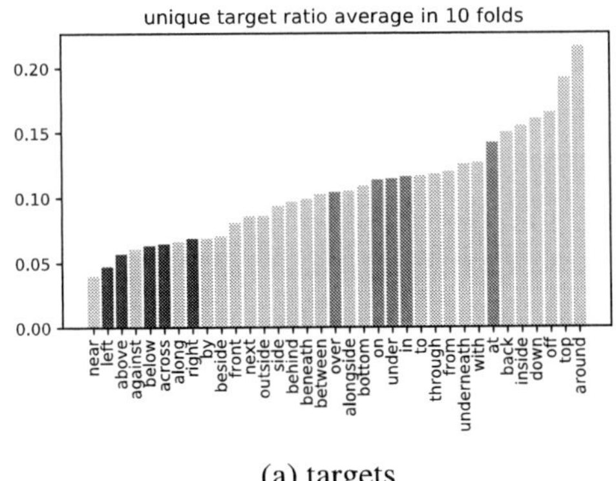
(a) targets

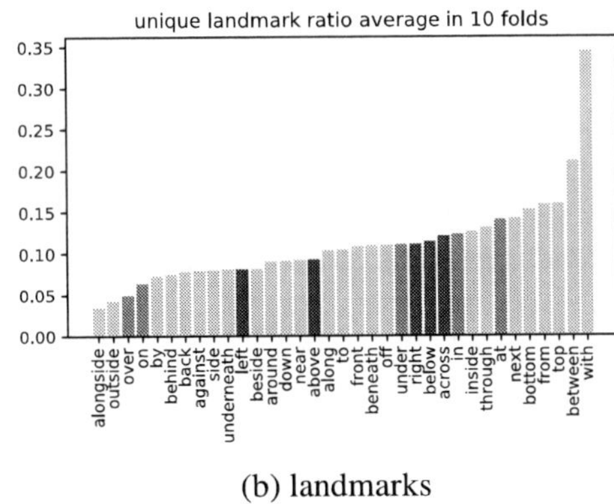
(b) landmarks

Figure 3: Ratio between unique types and all types per spatial relation in the balanced dataset for LM2.

Comparing Figure 4 with Figure 2 we first observe that the perplexity of LM2$'$ on the descriptions is overall several magnitudes lower than the perplexity of LM2 (max 0.06, max 140). Secondly, we observe that the perplexities of phrases containing different relations are very similar and that there is no separation of phrases by perplexity depending on the relation bias. The results are in line with our argument above. Knowing the landmark, it is much easier for the language model to predict the relation (of either kinds) and the target.

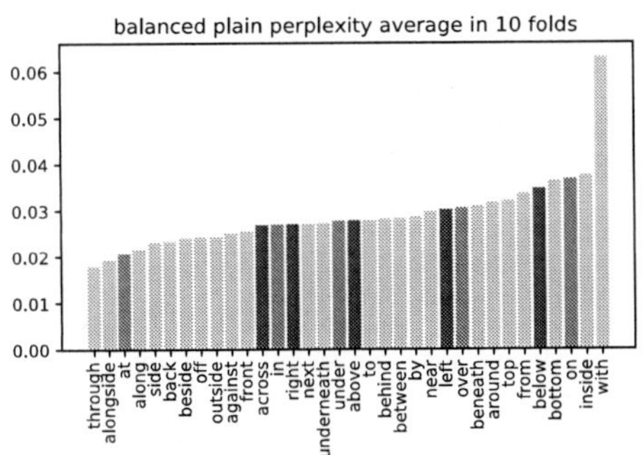

Figure 4: Mean perplexities of LM2$'$ by spatial relation (orange: functionally biased, blue: geometrically biased)

In conclusion, the explanation why descriptions with functionally-biased relations have a higher perplexity than descriptions with geometrically-biased descriptions appears to be twofold: (i) functionally-biased relations are more selective of their targets as expressed by the uniqueness counts, and (ii) functional relations are also more selective of their landmarks but this fact works against the performance of the language model.

As it is trained on the sequence left to right, it has to learn to predict relations only on the basis of targets which in the case of functionally-biased relations are represented by more unique tokens than geometrically-biased relations. The more informative words, the landmarks, that would enable the language model to predict a functional relation, comes last, after the relation has already been seen. The possible reason why geometrically-biased relations lead to lower perplexities of a language model on descriptions is because they have fewer unique targets. Hence, our Hypothesis 1 which linked selectivity of functionally-biased relations to low perplexity of phrases can be refuted. In spatial relations the order of the semantic interpretation of tokens (that we want to capture in these experiments) is different from the linear syntactic order of order which can be captured by the language model. When this order is changed as in LM2$'$ our predictions come closer to the hypothesis (Figure 4).[5]

By removing the frequency bias on spatial relations in LM2 we fix the distribution of spatial relations and examine the effect of distribution of targets and landmarks on perplexities of phrases (spatial relation as fixed context). In the following section, we fix the distributions of targets and landmarks of each spatial relation and examine the perplexity of phrases when another spatial relation is projected in this context (targets-landmarks as fixed context).

____

[5]Modulo that landmarks are, as discussed above, well-predictive of relations of both kinds.

5 Varying spatial relations

5.1 Hypotheses

Given a particular spatial relation, the distribution of targets and landmarks that occur with it creates a particular signature of targets and landmarks, the target-landmark context of a spatial relation. In this experiment, we investigate the effect on perplexity of phrases when another spatial relation is projected in such a target-landmark context. Given different selectivity of functionally- and geometrically-biased spatial relations, namely the functionally-based spatial relations are more selective of their targets and landmarks and therefore create more specific contexts, we should observe differences in perplexities of phrases when other spatial relations are projected in these contexts. In particular, we hypothesise that geometrically-biased spatial relations are more easily swappable than functionally-biased spatial relations as measured by the perplexity of a language model trained on the original, non-swapped phrases (Hypothesis 4).

5.2 Method

We use LM2 from Section 4 (trained on the balanced frequencies of spatial relations) with no additional training from the previous experiment. We group descriptions in the evaluation set by spatial relation. For each phrase containing a particular spatial relation, we replace it with every other spatial relation and estimate the perplexity of the resulting phrase using a language model. Finally, we calculate the mean of perplexities over all phrases. We use 10-fold cross-validation and report the final means across the 10 folds.

5.3 Results

Figure 5 shows a %-increase in mean complexities from those in Figure 2 when LM2 is applied on phrases with swapped relations in the contexts of the original relations. Hence, the column "at" shows the %-increase in perplexities of phrases that originally contained *at* in the validation dataset but this was replaced by all other spatial relations. Comparing with Figure 2 the estimated perplexities are higher across all cases which is predictable. There is a weak tendency that replacing functionally-biased relations with other relations leads to higher perplexities of spatial descriptions than replacing geometrically-biased relations, but the distinction is not clear cut

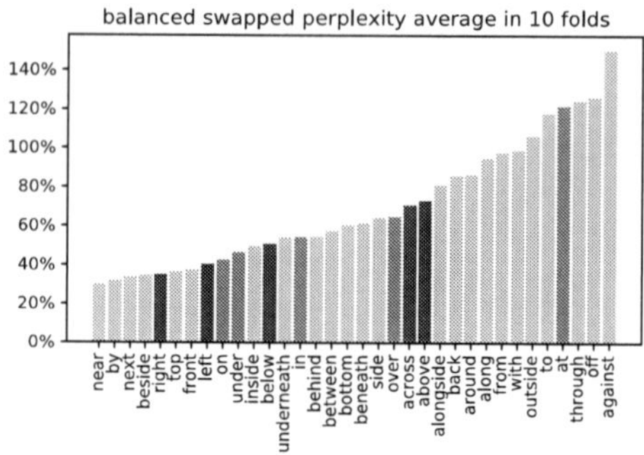

Figure 5: %-increase in perplexities of LM2 shown per context of the original preposition when swapped with another one.

(Hypothesis 4 partially confirmed). The lack of a clear distinction between two classes of descriptions confirms our previous observations about landmarks and targets: the LM has learned particular contexts for both kinds of descriptions.

6 Discussion and conclusion

We explored the degree that the functional and geometric character of spatial relations can be identified by a neural language model by focusing on spatial descriptions of controlled length and containing normalised relations. Our first question was about the implications of using a neural language model for this task. The previous research (Dobnik and Kelleher, 2013) used normalised entropy of target-landmarks per relation and log likelihood ratio between target-landmarks and relations to test this. These are focused measures that estimate the variation and the strength of association of words in a corpus. On the other hand, a language model provides a more general probabilistic representation of the entire description. As such it captures any kind of associations between words in a sequence. The other important observation is that it captures sequential relations in the direction left to right and as we have seen the sequential nature of the language model does not correspond precisely with the order in which semantic arguments of spatial relations are interpreted. However, nonetheless we can say that language models are able to capture a distinction between functional and geometric spatial relations (plus other semantic distinctions) to a similar degree of success as previously reported measures. Our initial hypothesis about the greater selectivity of spatial relations for its arguments is correct but it is exemplified in a greater perplexity of a language model in the context of balanced spatial relations. We argued that this has to do with the fact that the targets are more unique to these relations (which is consequence of a greater specificity for arguments of functionally biased relations) and is also related to the way a sequential language model works. In the unbalanced dataset, the perplexity of the language model is reversed (it is lower with functionally biased relations) because the specificity of targets to relations is boosted with greater frequency of functionally-biased relations. The fact that functionally-biased relations are more frequent is probably related to the fact that such descriptions are more informative than purely geometric ones if available for a particular pair of objects.

We can only report tendencies based on the perplexities of our language models as our conclusions. This is because the functional-geometric bias is graded, because the predictions are highly dependent on the quality and the size of the dataset, and because other semantic relations might also be expressed by this measure. We chose a large contemporary dataset of image descriptions because we hope that it contains a high proportion of prepositions used as spatial relations. However, there is no guarantee that all prepositions in this dataset are used this way. We observe that there is considerable variation of obtained values across the 10-folds of cross-validation and we report the mean values over all folds. As an illustration, in the supplementary material (Section A.2) we give an example of graphs from two intermediary folds.

Using a language model in this task we have also learned new insights about the way language models encode spatial relations in image descriptions. It has been pointed out (cf. (Kelleher and Dobnik, 2017) among others) that convolutional neural networks with an attention model are designed to detect objects whereas spatial relations between objects are likely to be predicted by the language model. In this work we show that language models are not only predicting the relation (which is expected) but are able to distinguish between different classes of relations thus encoding finer semantic distinctions. This tells us that language models are able to encode a surprising amount of information about world knowledge with a usual caveat that it is difficult to separate several strands of this knowledge.

The work can be extended in several ways. One way is to study dataset effects on the predicted results. Datasets with descriptions of robotic actions and instructions may be particularly promising as they focus on spatial uses. Different normalisations of spatial relations have a significant effect on the results. In this work composite spatial relations such *on the left side of* are normalised to simple spatial relations such as *left*. However, these could be treated as separate relations as difference between may exist. A more systematic examination of clusters of spatial relations would eventually tell us what other spatial relations not yet identified as functionally or geometrically biased have similar properties to those that have identified as such experimentally.

Acknowledgements

The research of Dobnik and Ghanimifard was supported by a grant from the Swedish Research Council (VR project 2014-39) for the establishment of the Centre for Linguistic Theory and Studies in Probability (CLASP) at Department of Philosophy, Linguistics and Theory of Science (FLoV), University of Gothenburg.

The research of Kelleher was supported by the ADAPT Research Centre. The ADAPT Centre for Digital Content Technology is funded under the SFI Research Centres Programme (Grant 13/RC/2106) and is co-funded under the European Regional Development Funds.

References

Yoshua Bengio, Réjean Ducharme, Pascal Vincent, and Christian Jauvin. 2003. A neural probabilistic language model. *Journal of machine learning research*, 3(Feb):1137–1155.

François Chollet et al. 2015. Keras. `https://github.com/keras-team/keras`.

Gordon Christie, Ankit Laddha, Aishwarya Agrawal, Stanislaw Antol, Yash Goyal, Kevin Kochersberger, and Dhruv Batra. 2016. Resolving language and vision ambiguities together: Joint segmentation & prepositional attachment resolution in captioned scenes. *arXiv*, 1604.02125 [cs.CV].

Kenny R Coventry and Simon C Garrod. 2004. *Saying, seeing, and acting: the psychological semantics of spatial prepositions*. Psychology Press, Hove, East Sussex.

Kenny R. Coventry, Mercè Prat-Sala, and Lynn Richards. 2001. The interplay between geometry and function in the apprehension of Over, Under, Above and Below. *Journal of Memory and Language*, 44(3):376–398.

Sebastien Delecraz, Alexis Nasr, Frederic Bechet, and Benoit Favre. 2017. Correcting prepositional phrase attachments using multimodal corpora. In *Proceedings of the 15th International Conference on Parsing Technologies*, pages 72–77, Pisa, Italy. Association for Computational Linguistics.

Simon Dobnik and John D. Kelleher. 2013. Towards an automatic identification of functional and geometric spatial prepositions. In *Proceedings of PRE-CogSsci 2013: Production of referring expressions – bridging the gap between cognitive and computational approaches to reference*, pages 1–6, Berlin, Germany.

Simon Dobnik and John D. Kelleher. 2014. Exploration of functional semantics of prepositions from corpora of descriptions of visual scenes. In *Proceedings of the Third V&L Net Workshop on Vision and Language*, pages 33–37, Dublin, Ireland. Dublin City University and the Association for Computational Linguistics.

Yarin Gal and Zoubin Ghahramani. 2016. A theoretically grounded application of dropout in recurrent neural networks. In *Advances in neural information processing systems*, pages 1019–1027.

Simon Garrod, Gillian Ferrier, and Siobhan Campbell. 1999. In and on: investigating the functional geometry of spatial prepositions. *Cognition*, 72(2):167–189.

Alex Graves, Abdel-rahman Mohamed, and Geoffrey Hinton. 2013. Speech recognition with deep recurrent neural networks. In *Acoustics, speech and signal processing (icassp), 2013 ieee international conference on*, pages 6645–6649. IEEE.

Michael Grubinger, Paul D. Clough, Henning Müller, and Thomas Deselaers. 2006. The IAPR benchmark: A new evaluation resource for visual information systems. In *Proceedings of OntoImage 2006: Workshop on language resources for content-based mage retrieval during LREC 2006*, Genoa, Italy. European Language Resources Association.

Annette Herskovits. 1986. *Language and spatial cognition: an interdisciplinary study of the prepositions in English*. Cambridge University Press, Cambridge.

John D. Kelleher and Fintan J. Costello. 2005. Cognitive representations of project prepositions. In *In Proceedings of the Second ACL-Sigsem Workshop on The Linguistic Dimensions of Prepositions and their Used In Computational Linguistic Formalisems and Applications*.

John D. Kelleher and Fintan J. Costello. 2009. Applying computational models of spatial prepositions to visually situated dialog. *Computational Linguistics*, 35(2):271–306.

John D. Kelleher and Simon Dobnik. 2017. What is not where: the challenge of integrating spatial representations into deep learning architectures. In *Proceedings of the Conference on Logic and Machine Learning in Natural Language (LaML 2017), Gothenburg, 12 –13 June*, volume 1 of *CLASP Papers in Computational Linguistics*, pages 41–52, Gothenburg, Sweden.

John D. Kelleher and Geert-Jan M. Kruijff. 2006. Incremental generation of spatial referring expressions in situated dialog. In *Proceedings of the 44th Annual Meeting of the Association for Computational Linguistics*, ACL-44, pages 1041–1048. Association for Computational Linguistics.

Diederik Kingma and Jimmy Ba. 2014. Adam: A method for stochastic optimization. In *International Conference on Learning Representations*.

Parisa Kordjamshidi, Taher Rahgooy, Marie-Francine Moens, James Pustejovsky, Umar Manzoor, and Kirk Roberts. 2017. CLEF 2017: Multimodal spatial role labeling (mSpRL) task overview. In *Experimental IR Meets Multilinguality, Multimodality, and Interaction*, pages 367–376, Cham. Springer International Publishing.

Parisa Kordjamshidi, Martijn Van Otterlo, and Marie-Francine Moens. 2011. Spatial role labeling: Towards extraction of spatial relations from natural language. *ACM Transactions on Speech and Language Processing*, 8(3):4:1–4:36.

Ranjay Krishna, Yuke Zhu, Oliver Groth, Justin Johnson, Kenji Hata, Joshua Kravitz, Stephanie Chen, Yannis Kalantidis, Li-Jia Li, David A Shamma, Michael Bernstein, and Li Fei-Fei. 2017. Visual genome: Connecting language and vision using crowdsourced dense image annotations. *International Journal of Computer Vision*, 123(1):32–73.

Barbara Landau. 1996. Multiple geometric representations of objects in languages and language learners. *Language and space*, pages 317–363.

Barbara Landau. 2016. Update on "What" and "where" in spatial language: A new division of labor for spatial terms. *Cognitive Science*, 41(S2):321–350.

Barbara Landau and Ray Jackendoff. 1993. "what" and "where" in spatial language and spatial cognition. *Behavioral and Brain Sciences*, 16(2):217–238, 255–265.

G.D. Logan and D.D. Sadler. 1996. A computational analysis of the apprehension of spatial relations. In M. Bloom, P.and Peterson, L. Nadell, and M. Garrett, editors, *Language and Space*, pages 493–529. MIT Press.

Tomáš Mikolov, Martin Karafiát, Lukáš Burget, Jan Černockỳ, and Sanjeev Khudanpur. 2010. Recurrent neural network based language model. In *Eleventh Annual Conference of the International Speech Communication Association*.

Arnau Ramisa, Josiah Wang, Ying Lu, Emmanuel Dellandrea, Francesc Moreno-Noguer, and Robert Gaizauskas. 2015. Combining geometric, textual and visual features for predicting prepositions in image descriptions. In *Proceedings of the 2015 Conference on Empirical Methods in Natural Language Processing*, pages 214–220, Lisbon, Portugal. Association for Computational Linguistics.

Cyrus Rashtchian, Peter Young, Micah Hodosh, and Julia Hockenmaier. 2010. Collecting image annotations using Amazon's Mechanical Turk. In *Proceedings of the NAACL HLT 2010 Workshop on creating speech and language data with Amazon's Mechanical Turk*, Los Angeles, CA. North American Chapter of the Association for Computational Linguistics (NAACL).

Gerard J Steen, Aletta G Dorst, J Berenike Herrmann, Anna Kaal, Tina Krennmayr, and Trijntje Pasma. 2010. *A method for linguistic metaphor identification: From MIP to MIPVU*, volume 14. John Benjamins Publishing.

A Supplementary material

A.1 Language Model Architecture

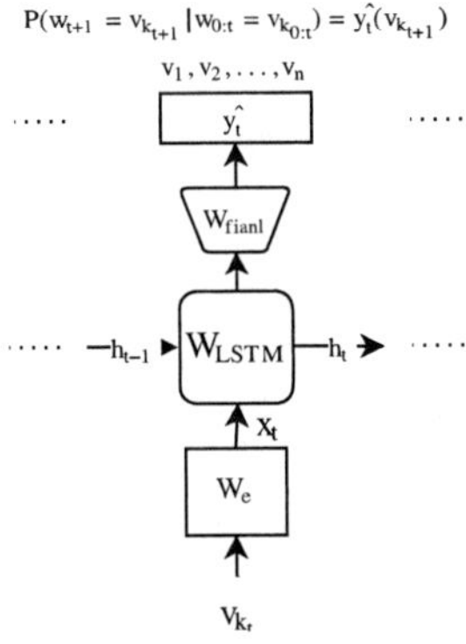

Figure 6: The recurrent language model diagram with LSTM recurrent unit.

The neural language model architecture with the Long-Short Terms Memory (LSTM) function and its parameters, similar to tied weights in (Gal and Ghahramani, 2016):

- $W_e \in R^{n \times d}$ for word embeddings,

- $W_{LSTM} \in R^{2d \times 4d}$ for parameters of the Long-Short Term Memory function,

- $W_{Final} \in R^{d \times n}$ of the final dense layer with *softmax*.

where n is the vocabulary size for $V = \{v_1, v_2, \ldots, v_n\}$ and d is both the embeddings size and the memory size in LSTM. For mini-batches from training data, these parameters are being updated using a stochastic gradient descent to minimise the loss.

$$x_t = \delta_{v_{k_t}} \cdot W_e \tag{5}$$

$$\begin{pmatrix} i \\ f \\ o \\ g \end{pmatrix} = \begin{pmatrix} \sigma \\ \sigma \\ \sigma \\ \tanh \end{pmatrix} \left(\begin{pmatrix} x_t \\ h_{t-1} \end{pmatrix} \cdot W_{LSTM} \right) \tag{6}$$

$$c_t = f \circ c_{t-1} + i \circ g \tag{7}$$

$$h_t = o \circ \tanh(c_t) \tag{8}$$

$$\hat{y}_t = \text{softmax}(h_t \cdot W_{final} + b) \tag{9}$$

where $\delta_{v_{k_t}}$ represents the one-hot encoding of the t-th word in the sequence. The x_t is the word embedding for this word, and two vectors c_t and h_t represent the states of the recurrent unit. Figure 6 illustrates the same equation.

A.2 Evaluation

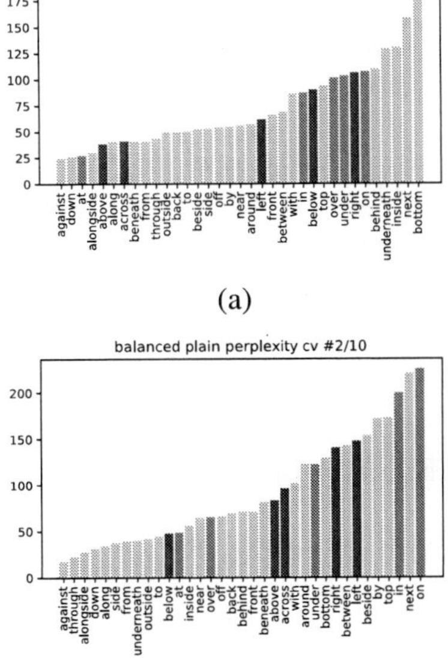

(a)

(b)

Figure 7: Mean perplexities of LM2 by spatial relation for (a) folds 1 and (b) 2 (orange: functionally biased, blue: geometrically biased).

Building and Learning Structures in a Situated Blocks World Through Deep Language Understanding

Ian Perera[1], James F. Allen[1,2], Choh Man Teng[1], Lucian Galescu[1]
[1]Institute for Human and Machine Cognition, Pensacola, FL 32502 USA
[2]University of Rochester, Department of Computer Science, Rochester, NY 14627 USA
`iperera@ihmc.us, jallen@ihmc.us, cmteng@ihmc.us, lgalescu@ihmc.us`

Abstract

We demonstrate a system for understanding natural language utterances for structure description and placement in a situated blocks world context. By relying on a rich, domain-specific adaptation of a generic ontology and a logical form structure produced by a semantic parser, we obviate the need for an intermediate, domain-specific representation and can produce a reasoner that grounds and reasons over concepts and constraints with real-valued data. This linguistic base enables more flexibility in interpreting natural language expressions invoking intrinsic concepts and features of structures and space. We demonstrate some of the capabilities of a system grounded in deep language understanding and present initial results in a structure learning task.

1 Introduction

Even as early as one of the first Blocks World natural language interaction systems, SHRDLU (Winograd, 1971), discussions about structures and space have been viewed as the foundation for future language understanding systems dealing with more abstract and higher-level concepts. Since then, the field has advanced in the task of learning how to understand utterances in Blocks World and other situated environments by using statistical methods grounding syntactic trees to entities and actions in the world to learn placement descriptions (Bisk et al., 2016), predicates (Kollar et al., 2013), actions (Kim and Mooney, 2012; She et al., 2014) or a combination of paths and actions (Tellex et al., 2011). However, rather than considering grounding solely as a mapping to actions and objects in the world, we use the deep language understanding capabilities of the TRIPS parser (Allen et al., 2008) to find deeper conceptual connections to primitive, composable, and often recursive aspects of structures, and use this knowledge to better understand conceptually-rich utterances without the need for training data. Inspired by the cognitive linguistic theory of conceptual mappings (Fauconnier, 1997), we focus on projection mappings between structure and set features and demonstrate instances of common situated language that makes use of such mappings. With these concepts grounded in a situated space, we believe we will be poised to extend the concepts in Blocks World into more abstract reasoning and language through grounded metaphor.

We also demonstrate the ability of our system to build up a model of a class of structures through natural language dialogue. Rather than constructing a new domain-specific representation for storing such knowledge, as in work by Hixon et al. (2015), we retain the semantic logical form structure as our base representation, using ontological concepts of comparison and semantic argument structures to ground concepts and predicates in the situated environment. We therefore aim to show that a linguistic structures from a semantic parser can serve as a strong base for reasoning and model-building in a situated context.

2 Capabilities and Tasks

We evaluate our system in a situated blocks world environment with 6-inch cubes placed on a table. Aside from unique identifiers for tracking, each cube is considered identical. Our physical apparatus consists of two Kinect 2.0's aimed at the table, with the multiple Kinects helping to avoid issues with block occlusion. The depth information is used to recognize and process position and rotation information that is then relayed to the system. Currently only block position is used, but orientation information is also recorded.

For user-system interaction, there is a screen at the end of the table across from the user which dis-

Proceedings of the First International Workshop on Spatial Language Understanding (SpLU-2018), pages 12–20
New Orleans, Louisiana, June 6, 2018. ©2018 Association for Computational Linguistics

plays an avatar that can speaks system-generated utterances and display it on-screen. The avatar can also point to blocks or locations on the table, although we do not use this functionality in our dialogues. When the system wants to place a block or provide an example structure, it generates a 3D image of the blocks overlaid with the existing scene that can be presented to the user or an assistant that will then place the blocks in the appropriate location. An image of the apparatus is shown in Figure 1.

Figure 1: The apparatus used to interact with the system.

We focus on two tasks for evaluating our system within the context of a natural language dialogue system. The first is correctly understanding a variety of natural placement utterances and generating the expected placement of blocks that satisfies the command. There has been significant previous work on learning to interpret typical placement instructions (Bisk et al., 2016; Misra et al., 2017; Wang et al., 2016) or descriptions of block scenes (Bisk et al., 2018). While we have limited capabilities for understanding such instructions, this prior work is better suited for more robust and precise placement interaction that does not utilize conceptual composition. Therefore, rather than solely understanding simple phrases such as "Place a block on top of the leftmost block", we focus our efforts towards understanding more complex phrases that utilize context, such as "Add another one," and linguistic/semantic composition, as in, "Place three towers in a row with increasing height".

The second task is teaching the system to learn a class of structures by providing it with a set of constraints. The user is provided with a number of positive and negative visual examples of a class of structures to learn (akin to resolving a Bongard problem (Bongard et al., 1970)), and once they have determined the underlying constraints of the structures, they must engage in a dialogue with the system to teach it the structure class so that it will be able to recognize structures belonging to that class. This task importantly differs from the first task and prior situated language understanding work in that the user is not communicating a specific goal structure to be achieved by the user through placement actions, but instead providing a set of general constraints and concepts that admit a number of possible structures.

3 System Architecture

We build upon the TRIPS architecture (Allen et al., 2001), which connects a number of components through message passing, with each component able to be tailored to a particular domain.

3.1 Semantic Extraction

The first component that sees user language input is the domain-general, rules-based TRIPS parser that is backed by a domain-generic ontology augmented with domain-specific concepts, such as blocks, rows, and columns. The output from the parser is a logical form semantic graph with a number of possible speech acts. This output is then passed to the Interpretation Manager (IM), which determines the appropriate speech act given dialogue context and further refines roles and interpretations according to domain-specific rules and ontological constraints.

3.2 Problem Solving Act Generation

Next, the output of the IM is processed by the Collaborative Problem Solving Agent, a central module that facilitates the acts that make up collaborative problem solving (i.e. the joint task actions carried out by the user and system). It passes the output to the Collaborative State Manager (CSM) to generate and store a new goal, query, or assertion. The appropriate act is then sent to the Behavioral Agent (BA), tasked with reasoning and acting in the environment. If the system has a query or goal proposal for the user, the message passing works in reverse, with the goal or query added to the goal hierarchy stored in the CSM. The current goal or query provides a context for resolving future utterances, providing additional information to aid in choosing the appropriate speech act.

3.3 Application to Tasks

In the structure building task, we primarily make use of the goal and sub-goal mechanisms to provide actions to the BA so that it can act in the environment towards the desired structure. The user can also provide assertions containing definitions of substructures to be used in the building process. In the structure learning task, we primarily process assertions that describe the general properties of the structure type, and queries to ask the user about properties or ask for an example. The task to be completed is determined by the user specifying the goal as the first utterance (e.g., "I want to build a staircase" versus "I want to teach you what a staircase is"). This top-level goal provides additional context for utterance resolution. For example, the utterance "The left-most block must be on top" would be processed as a proposed goal in the structure building task (as it describes a difference between the current and desired state), but as an assertion in the structure learning task (as it describes a property that should generally hold).

4 Semantic Logical Form Backing

Rather than convert semantic information from the semantic output of a domain-general parser, we directly use the semantic output of the TRIPS parser (backed by a combination of a domain-general and domain-specific ontology) as the underlying logical representation for assertions, constraints, and commands. This backing is enabled by a number of features specific to the output of the TRIPS parser. First, the ontology provides a method to generalize multiple related utterances or fragments to a single interpretation to be conveyed to the reasoning agent and handled similarly. Second, the semantic output of the TRIPS parser includes an ontology and tree-based representation of scales, which makes feature comparisons explicit and provides units for evaluating scales using the appropriate metric. Finally, the semantic roles (*figure* for head properties, and *ground* for reference properties) provide a more nuanced level of comparison among object and structure features than typical semantic parsers focused on events and higher-level interactions among people. For example, the sentence, "The left column is taller than the rightmost column," taller resolves to a concept ONT::MORE-VAL (enabling a simple operator extraction), with a *scale* of ONT::HEIGHT-SCALE, a *figure* of "the left column", and a *ground* of "the rightmost column".

Developing and relying on the semantic structure for reasoning provides a long-term advantage for extending the physical domain to handle reasoning in different domains or at a more abstract level. Currently, the structures used to tie the semantic structures to the domain could easily be extended to other domains simply by modifying the interpretation of predicates and generating new features, while referring expression and dialogue processing can remain largely unchanged. A metaphorical reasoning system, for example, could make use of the same semantic structures and simply modify the reasoning environment and generate inference from a physical simulation or concrete projection of abstract concepts, and could borrow predicates and features from Blocks World.

5 Predicates

Predicates describe binary positional aspects relating a block or structure to a particular context. All predicates have at least one argument, the subject, but typically also admit a context (e.g., other blocks, or the rest of the scene). For example, even though the *top* predicate may seem to take only one argument, we resolve it using a second argument that contains the complement of the scene (in the case of "the top block") or a contrast set (in the case of "the top block of the left column"). Predicates are used both for referring expressions to choose a particular group of blocks and for applying constraints to structure properties and placement instructions. For example, the command "the top block must be on the left" uses a predicate for both the referring expression (*the top block*) and a constraint on its location (*on the left*).

Rather than defining logical formulas for evaluating predicates, our predicates are designed programmatically using real-valued coordinates in 3D space with an emphasis on relations dealing with a vertical 2D plane between the user and the system's viewpoint. They are evaluated either by comparing positions and dimensions over the quantification of the blocks in the structures or over axis-aligned bounding boxes encapsulating the blocks. For example, the predicate $above(a,b)$ requires that the x- and y-coordinate extents of the bounding boxes of the a and b intersect and that the minimum z-coordinate value of a is greater than the maximum z-value of b (with z being the vertical dimension). Each predicate is mapped to one or more TRIPS ontological concepts for evaluating when such a predicate appears in the logical form. The ontology is specific enough that no concept could yield more than one predicate interpretation. All predicates also include tolerances to account for real-world variations in the input data, but because of the nature of the depth data and the known size of the blocks, there is little noise in the positions of the blocks.

6 Features

The term "features" in the context of Blocks World refers to all quantifiable aspects of blocks and block arrangements. However, we also extend this definition to include potential ways of perceiving, discussing, or processing blocks and groups of blocks. For example, a set of blocks could be considered as a column, a row with or without a particular ordering, or simply a set of blocks with no relation to each other. The values of such features can be integers, real numbers, vectors, or an arrangement. Furthermore, arrangements can have multiple features assigned to them forming a feature group. For example, a sequence arrangement can generate a row feature, a column feature, the count of the number of blocks or structures within, an origin as a vector, and a direction as a vector.

6.1 Feature Mention Extraction

Given the semantic parser output, the reasoning agent parses the features described in multiple passes. First, referring expressions are extracted by finding mentions of objects that the reasoning agent knows how to recognize or instantiate in the environment (i.e., blocks, rows, columns, and spaces), and then storing constraints according to modifiers on its location (represented using predicates). Next, the features are extracted from the same parse tree, which typically contains a feature name as an arrangement name (e.g., a column), a scale (e.g., width-scale), or a number (e.g., the number of blocks in the specified set). Finally, the relevant operator (e.g., less than, at least, equal to) is extracted and sets up the constraint on the values or referenced features mentioned. In certain cases, the TRIPS parser explicitly provides the comparator (e.g., providing an ONT::MIN concept and appropriate arguments for "at least"), and in other cases, the comparator and its arguments must be inferred by the appearance of sets with a specified size parameter.

While certain features, like the size of a set, have an explicitly defined value, we also generate features that have an implicit value that may not be meaningful to the user. For example, linearity can take a value from 0-1 based on the deviation of the elements from a line of best fit. If the user states, "The bottom blocks must be in a line", we calculate the value and compare against a threshold to determine whether the constraint holds, or can compare using an operator against the linearity of another set of blocks. Features of this type are often difficult to explain linguistically or symbolically, and thus lean more on specific visual processing and could be tied to statistical computer vision models in the future.

6.2 Structure Models and Constraint Satisfaction

In the structure learning task, the system learns a set of constraints that describes a structure. As the goal is to teach the system a general concept rather than describe one particular instance, the learned constraints apply as rules that will apply in various configurations, rather than applying to particular blocks currently on the table. Therefore, referring expressions in the constraints for a model are reevaluated each time a particular instance is tested. We currently process four types of constraints: feature, predicate, structure, and existential constraints. Feature constraints, describe a property (such as width or height) that generally holds for the structure as a whole, such as "The height is at least 3 blocks". Predicate constraints enforce that a particular set of blocks satisfy a particular predicate (e.g., "The leftmost column is next to the center column"). Structural constraints enforce that the blocks referred to by a referring expression obeys a feature constraint (e.g., "The leftmost column has at least 3 blocks"). Predicate and structure constraints can also be modified to be satisfied if they are exclusively satisfied by only one grounding of an object type in a referring expression (e.g., "Only the leftmost column has a height greater than 2").

7 Recursive and Compositional Feature Understanding

Recursive and composition representations of features are essential for deep language understanding even in the simplified environment of Blocks

Ontological Concept	Lemmas	# of Arguments
ONT::ABOVE	above	2
W::HIGHER	higher	2
ONT::BELOW	below, beneath, under, underneath	2
W::LOWER	lower	2
ONT::ADJACENT	adjacent (to), next to, beside, by, contiguous (with), flush	2
ONT::CONNECTED	abut, adjoin, connect, touch	1,2
W::TOGETHER	together	1,2
ONT::ON	on, on top of	2
ONT::LEVEL	level with	1,2
ONT::TOP-LOC...	top	1,2
ONT::MIDDLE-LOC...	middle	(1),2
ONT::BOTTOM-LOC...	bottom	1,2
ONT::BETWEEN	(in) between	2
ONT::CENTER	center	(1),2
ONT::LEFT-LOC	left, lefthand, leftmost	(1),2
ONT::RIGHT-LOC	right, righthand, rightmost	(1),2
W::ANYWHERE	anywhere	1

Table 1: The list of predicates understood by the system, with their concept in the TRIPS ontology, the matching lemmas that can resolve to that concept during parsing (designated by hand or from WordNet mappings (Miller, 1995)), and the number of arguments each predicate can take. An argument number in parentheses indicates that the second argument, the reference, is inferred to be the scene complement of the first argument. Predicates like ONT::CONNECTED admit sets of blocks as their single argument.

Ontological Concept	Data Type
ONT::WIDTH-SCALE	real+, count
ONT::HEIGHT-SCALE	real+, count
ONT::LENGTH-SCALE	real+, count
ONT::CENTER	point
ONT::LOCATION	point
ONT::STARTPOINT	point
ONT::ENDPOINT	point
ONT::TOP-LOC...	point
ONT::BOTTOM-LOC...	point
ONT::NUMBER	count
ONT::COL-FORMATION	column
ONT::ROW-FORMATION	row
ONT::DIRECTION	vector
ONT::HORIZONTAL	(real+)
ONT::VERTICAL	(real+)
ONT::LINE	(real+)

Table 2: The features generated by the system for blocks, sets of blocks, and sequences, listed by their concept in the TRIPS ontology and the resulting data type. A data type in parentheses indicates the value is not presented to the user but is compared against thresholds or other sets of blocks.

World. Take for example the utterance "lengthen the first column of the row by 2". Such an utterance refers to multiple features both for identifying the relevant set of blocks and for the desired action. However, beyond identifying the set of relevant blocks, it also enforces a conceptual model on the blocks that is necessary for the interpretation of "lengthen", which requires a sequence rather than a set. Similarly, the notion of "first" implies an ordering of the row, taken in reading order (left-to-right) unless another context, such as a specified placement order, overwrites it.

The fact that these representations arise from simple interactions and often without explicit definition motivates our notion of such concepts as "features". Thus in the above example, the placement of the blocks admits a "row" feature group consisting of a direction, a length, and a sequence of "column" features, each also having a sequence of blocks (which itself has a length feature) and an upward direction, as well as a "height".

We also represent the composition of these features for utterances such as "place the columns in a row with increasing height". Our main method for composition is projection, which in this context we take to mean the reduction of features (with the number of features being the dimensionality of the concept) to enable composition with other features of the appropriate type. In this case, the phrase "increasing height" generates an increasing sequence of integers which is then projected onto the row to replace the individual height features of each of its constituent columns, generating the desired structure. Note that while the row itself could have a height as a structure as a whole, this single value would not be compatible with the sequence. This process is illustrated in Figure 2.

The example in Figure 2 also illustrates the advantage of such a technique in providing robustness in the face of linguistic ambiguity. For example, the "increasing height" could be modifying the placement of the columns, the columns themselves, or, as the TRIPS parser outputs, the row. Because of the restrictions on projection, we can correctly apply the modification to the relevant features even when the target of the modification is not directly modifiable in a way that parallels the semantic interpretation. In some cases, the ontological interpretation of projection-indicating terms differ from our interpretation, and such information must be discarded. For example, while the parser may extract the ONT::IN-LOC concept from the word "in", in the above example the ONT::MANNER concept is more appropriate. The projection restrictions allow us to determine the correct sense regardless of the specific concept while not being strictly dependent on the lemma.

7.1 Conceptual Features and Context

Moving away from the notion of sets as the only output of a referring expression confers an additional benefit in providing context for placement actions. Take, for example, the utterance "add another one". Treating the current set of blocks as a set of blocks would not provide the intended location of the next block (or group of blocks). To interpret such an utterance, we make use of discourse context, goal context, and the conceptual context of the last command. If the previous command involved an ordered sequence of some type of structure, "add another one" would make use of the conceptual context of the sequence which should be appended. In the case of a row, for example, we would pick the last element in the sequence, and place a duplicate in the next point when the direction vector is extended.

In certain cases, the conceptual context may not be available or sufficient. If the last utterance was "Place a block on top of the row", then "another one" might refer to either another block on top of the row or a block on top of the just placed block. In this case, we can make use of the overarching goal context. If the system is aware that the user is building a tower, increasing the height of the structure would be the expected next step. The system can make use of this context even without explicitly knowing the process for building a tower if the user provides a definition of the structure (e.g., "A tower is a structure taller than its diameter"), by choosing actions which bring the constraints closer to satisfaction.

8 Simulation and Querying Capabilities

While our system does not include a planner, we can nevertheless create a structure according to a set of constraints provided that the structure conforms to a grid-based structure. We generate a set of multiple iterations with blocks randomly dropped in a grid with the size determined either by default dimensions or constrained by global features of width and height. Once we find an arrangement that satisfies the constraints, we return the structure to the user to ask if the example is correct. In the 2D plane, the number of possible structures is constrained enough to generate an example satisfying the constraints in real-time. While we can then provide this structure to the user or assistant in the 3D view, we currently do not support generation of natural language descriptions for the placement of each block.

The system is also able to generate questions about structures when learning, in order to extract clear constraints from the user. When appropriate in dialogue, the system generates a random underspecified constraint that has not yet been mentioned, typically concerning general features (e.g., width or height), or more specific constraints (e.g., the placement restrictions of the top block). Specific constraints dealing with specific structures are generated based on user examples. For example, the system would ask about the placement of the top block only if there was a single top block in a previously shown example. In our architecture, we are then able to interpret a response fragment, fill the constraint parameters, and add the constraint to the model. We find that such questions greatly increase the quality of the user's given con-

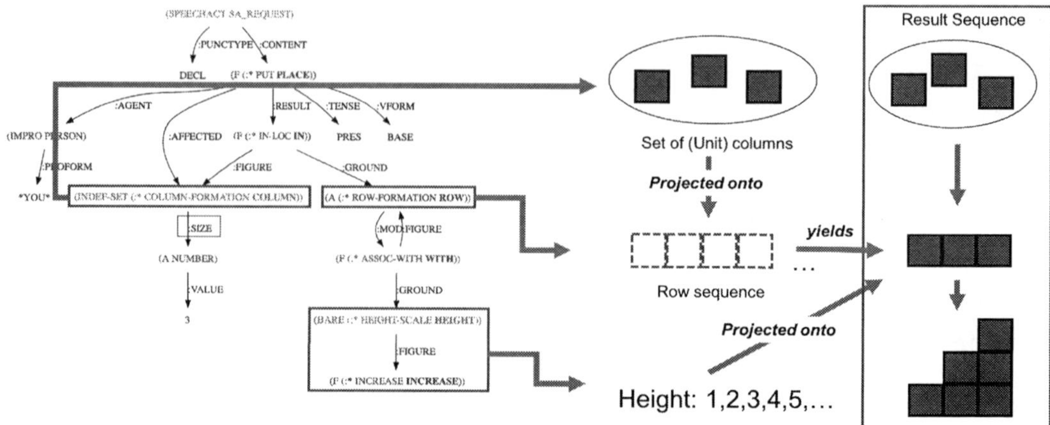

Figure 2: An example of the projection processing for the utterance "Place three columns in a row with increasing height." The features (boxed in the parse tree) are extracted and used to generate new individual instances with appropriate features. The columns are then projected into the appropriate feature of the row, and the height sequence projects onto the row of columns to create the final structure.

straints, as the questions provide an example of the types of constraints the system is most capable of handling and provide guidance for the user in organizing their conception of the structure class.

9 Evaluation

Currently evaluation is in preliminary stages, with an emphasis on expanding capabilities in terms of the variety of structures able to be built and recognized. A comprehensive evaluation task can be difficult for this system, given its symbolic backing. As there is no statistical learning, the usefulness of the system is primarily determined by the coverage of understood linguistic constructions at two levels – at the semantic parser level and at the level of interpretation given a correct semantic parse. One challenge faced in accurately evaluating the system is that users in a dialogue can be biased to choose language that the system understands, thereby reducing the average expressivity and linguistic complexity of their utterances. To partially address this, we have begun evaluations of our structure learning task, as we believe this task better illustrates the variety of language used to describe spatial concepts and structures, compared to the structure building task, which often consists solely of simple "place a block ⟨location⟩" utterances. Users are provided with positive and negative examples of a structure class (Figure 3) and must teach the system the concept.

Our initial evaluation to determine possible areas of improvement before actual trials began with

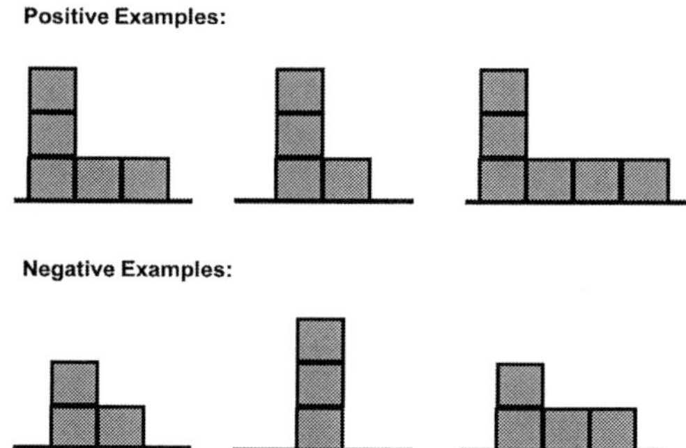

Figure 3: In the structure learning task, the user must determine the patterns followed by the positive examples that do not match the negative examples and explain these constraints to the system.

Wizard of Oz experiments. An advantage of a Wizard of Oz task is that the user maintains the complexity of their utterances as they see positive results from their descriptions, providing us with valuable insight into the various types of utterances our system must understand. We conducted 3 tasks with each of the 3 participants who were unaware of the details of the project, yielding 90 user utterances. A researcher took the place of the system by asking questions and presenting examples. By using a tablet that generated common questions and responses to be spoken by the avatar, these experiments could be carried out without the participants aware of the researcher's role as a stand-in for the system. To evaluate the system's performance at the semantic parser level, we ran the parser on the users' utterances in these experiments and correctly parsed 89% of the utterances. In evaluating the grounded interpretation level, we determine which of the correct parsed trees yield the desired constraint. Of the correctly parsed utterances, 90% yielded the desired constraint in the current state of the system with some development occurring after these trials. Further testing is required once the system's capabilities are finalized to see the performance of the system in an unrestricted setting with new users. Typical failures of the grounded interpretation level of the system involve utterances containing ordinal references (e.g., the second column), multiple values for constraints, ranges for feature values, or negative examples. All of these system abilities are near-future work. During this evaluation we also found that dialogue actions such as asking about features greatly simplified user utterances and therefore improved performance.

We also have begun trials of the complete dialogue system with promising results. The system is able to understand a number of different structure classes through dialogue, such as a staircase, an L shape, and a U shape. An example dialogue is shown in Figure 4, where the user was presented with the visual examples in Figure 3.

User: I want to teach you a shape.
System: Okay. Can you tell me something about the structure?
User: The bottom row must be at least 2.
System: Hmm, I didn't quite get that.
User: The bottom row has at least 2 blocks.
System: Okay. What is the greatest the width can be?
User: 5.
System: Okay, got it. Can you show me an example?
User: Yes. This is an example. ⟨*user shows example*⟩
System: Okay. Where can the top block be?
User: The top block is always on the left.
System: Okay.
User: ⟨*user builds example*⟩ Is this right?
System: I think so, because the bottom row's number is greater than or equal to 2 and the width is less than or equal to 5 and the top block is on the left.

Figure 4: A user dialogue taken from initial runs of the evaluation.

10 Future Work

We plan to continue working towards improving robustness in evaluations, implementing new ways of discussing structure building and structural constraints, and providing more dialogue actions to guide the user through their explanation and deal with errors or misunderstood assertions. In addition, we will be creating a database of predicate and feature definitions with multimodal groundings to begin our long-term goal of extending these physical groundings of concepts into abstract domains. Currently the TRIPS architecture is used as a base for a number of domains involving dialogue-assisted creation, such as biological models, music composition, and automated movie direction, and therefore provides a strong base for extending such concepts.

11 Acknowledgements

This work is supported by the DARPA CwC program and the DARPA Big Mechanism program under ARO contract W911NF-14-1-0391. Special thanks to SRI for their work in developing the physical apparatus, including block detection and avatar software.

References

J. Allen, Mary Swift, and Will de Beaumont. 2008. Deep Semantic Analysis of Text. In *Symposium on Semantics in Systems for Text Processing (STEP)*, pages 343–354, Morristown, NJ, USA. Association for Computational Linguistics.

James Allen, George Ferguson, and Amanda Stent. 2001. An architecture for more realistic conversational systems. In *Proceedings of the 6th international conference on Intelligent user interfaces - IUI '01*, pages 1–8.

Yonatan Bisk, Kevin J Shih, Yejin Choi, and Daniel Marcu. 2018. Learning Interpretable Spatial Operations in a Rich 3D Blocks World. In *Proceedings of the 32th AAAI Conference on Artificial Intelligence*.

Yonatan Bisk, Deniz Yuret, and Daniel Marcu. 2016. Natural Language Communication with Robots. *Proceedings of the 2016 Conference of the North American Chapter of the Association for Computational Linguistics: Human Language Technologies*, pages 751–761.

M. M. (Mikhail Moiseevich) Bongard, Joseph K. Hawkins, and Theodore Cheron. 1970. *Pattern recognition*. Spartan Books.

Gilles. Fauconnier. 1997. *Mappings in Thought and Language*. Cambridge University Press.

Ben Hixon, Peter Clark, and Hannaneh Hajishirzi. 2015. Learning Knowledge Graphs for Question Answering through Conversational Dialog. *NAACL*, pages 851–861.

Joohyun Kim and Raymond J Mooney. 2012. Unsupervised PCFG Induction for Grounded Language Learning with Highly Ambiguous Supervision. In *Proceedings of the Conference on Empirical Methods in Natural Language Processing and Natural Language Learning (EMNLP-CoNLL '12)*, July, pages 433–444.

Thomas Kollar, Jayant Krishnamurthy, and Grant Strimel. 2013. Toward interactive grounded language acquisition. In *Robotics: Science and Systems (RSS)*.

George A. Miller. 1995. WordNet: a lexical database for English. *Communications of the ACM*, 38(11):39–41.

Dipendra Misra, John Langford, and Yoav Artzi. 2017. Mapping Instructions and Visual Observations to Actions with Reinforcement Learning. In *Proceedings of the 2017 Conference on Empirical Methods in Natural Language Processing*, pages 1004–1015.

Lanbo She, Shaohua Yang, Yu Cheng, Yunyi Jia, Joyce Y Chai, and Ning Xi. 2014. Back to the Blocks World: Learning New Actions through Situated Human-Robot Dialogue. *Proceedings of the SIGDIAL 2014 Conference*, (June):89–97.

Stefanie Tellex, Thomas Kollar, and Steven Dickerson. 2011. Understanding Natural Language Commands for Robotic Navigation and Mobile Manipulation. *AAAI*.

Sida I Wang, Percy Liang, and Christopher D Manning. 2016. Learning Language Games through Interaction. In *The 54th Annual Meeting of the Association for Computational Linguistics*, pages 2368–2378.

Terry Winograd. 1971. Procedures as a Representation for Data in a Computer for Understanding Natural Language. Technical report, Massachusetts Institute of Technology Artificial Intelligence.

Computational Models for Spatial Prepositions

Georgiy Platonov
Department of Computer Science
University of Rochester
gplatono@cs.rochester.edu

Lenhart Schubert
Department of Computer Science
University of Rochester
schubert@cs.rochester.edu

Abstract

Developing computational models of spatial prepositions (such as *on, in, above, etc.*) is crucial for such tasks as human-machine collaboration, story understanding, and 3D model generation from descriptions. However, these prepositions are notoriously vague and ambiguous, with meanings depending on the types, shapes and sizes of entities in the argument positions, the physical and task context, and other factors. As a result truth value judgments for prepositional relations are often uncertain and variable. In this paper we treat the modeling task as calling for assignment of probabilities to such relations as a function of multiple factors, where such probabilities can be viewed as estimates of whether humans would judge the relations to hold in given circumstances. We implemented our models in a 3D blocks world and a room world in a computer graphics setting, and found that true/false judgments based on these models do not differ much more from human judgments that the latter differ from one another. However, what really matters pragmatically is not the accuracy of truth value judgments but whether, for instance, the computer models suffice for identifying objects described in terms of prepositional relations, (e.g., *the box to the left of the table*, where there are multiple boxes). For such tasks, our models achieved accuracies above 90% for most relations.

1 Introduction

Spatial prepositions are pervasive in natural languages and, therefore, interpretation and understanding of their meaning is critical to tasks involving NLP. The computational challenges are aggravated by the versatility and vagueness of these prepositions, and their sensitivity to miscellaneous factors such as shapes, sizes and salience of the relata, part-of relations, typicality, etc. *On* provides a good example of such semantically rich prepositions. When we say that one object is on another one, we strongly imply the relation of physical support between them. But support relations can be quite subtle, and can occur in diverse physical configurations:

Example 1

 a. a book on a shelf,
 b. a picture on a wall,
 c. a shirt on a person,
 d. a lamp on a post,
 e. a paragraph on a printed page,
 f. a fish on a hook,
 g. a sail on a ship,
 h. a fly on the ceiling.

In and *over* provide additional examples of semantically subtle, versatile prepositions. While it is conceivable that the diverse meanings of these prepositions are unrelated and arose from disparate communicative and historical pressures, there are strong arguments that this is not the case (Tyler and Evans, 2003). In fact, it is very likely that all or most of the different meanings associated with a preposition are based on some underlying primary meaning from which they all originated. In the case of *on*, it seems plausible that the initial meaning was essentially support by a more or less horizontal surface, which was then extended to further support relations, and metaphorized to nonspatial relations during the evolution of language. Because of this richness, it seems that no single criterion can capture all the instances where relations such as *on, in, over*, etc., hold.

However, there are three considerations that prompted us to proceed with the design of intuitive computational models of some of the most prevalent spatial prepositions: First, while no simple mathematical criterion can characterize any

Proceedings of the First International Workshop on Spatial Language Understanding (SpLU-2018), pages 21–30
New Orleans, Louisiana, June 6, 2018. ©2018 Association for Computational Linguistics

one of these relations, we can identify prototypical cases where the relations hold, and by considering such cases one by one, we can also zero in on non-geometrical factors that affect "truth" judgments in these cases. Second, people's judgments about whether a prepositional relation holds in a given case can be quite variable; therefore it should suffice to provide models that estimate the probability that arbitrary judges would consider the relation to hold. This approach is aligned with a view of predicate vagueness as variability in applicability judgments (Kyburg, 2000; Lassiter and Goodman, 2017), enabling Bayesian interpretation. And third, the ultimate success criterion in assessing models of prepositional predicates should be pragmatic; i.e, in physical settings we often use such predicates to identify a referent (*the blue book in front of the laptop*) or to specify a goal (*put the laptop on the table*), so our models should allow a natural language system to interpret such usages as a human would. Our results for referent identification suggest that our current models are nearly good enough for such purposes in various "blocks world" and "room world" configurations.

In developing a conceptual framework for modeling several common prepositional relations, we tried to achieve a trade-off: On one hand, we tried to avoid overcomplicating the model, keeping the number of primitive concepts used in the framework to a minimum. On the other, we strove to make the framework general enough to cover a wide range of objects and configurations.

In the following sections, we discuss related work, and then outline our modeling framework by examining the primitive concepts that are used as building blocks, and showing how these concepts come together in modeling a specific preposition. We then evaluate our approach in two test domains, a blocks world and a "room world", making use of Blender graphics software. We show that our computational models judge the chosen prepositional relations accurately enough in both worlds to enable rather good referent identification in relation to independent human judgments. We summarize our contributions, and directions for future work, in the concluding section.

2   Related work

Understanding the essence of the spatial prepositions is a major, long-standing task from NLP,

linguistic and cognitive science perspectives. Attempts to develop a computational model for spatial prepositions date back to the late 60s. The earliest attempts followed mainly geometric intuitions, relying on the concepts of contiguity, surface, etc. (Cooper, 1968). However, an impressively thorough study emerged in the 80s (Herskovits, 1985). Herskovits' analysis identified a variety of important factors that influence correctness judgments in the application of spatial prepositions, illustrating these factors with many striking examples (e.g., the role of object types and typicality in contrasts such as *the house on the lake* vs. **the truck on the lake*, or the role of the Figure/Ground distinction and object size and type in contrasts like *The bicycle is near Mary's house* vs. **Mary's house is near the bicycle*). Herskovits also proposed various abstract principles constraining the meaning and use of spatial prepositions. Compared to her study, our work is more narrowly focused on a few prepositions and two kinds of "worlds", but is distinguished by our emphasis on developing a computational model capable of actually evaluating the truth of prepositional relations in the chosen worlds.

A quite distinctive approach based on topology arose in 90s. A number of methodologies rooted in this idea were aimed at spatial reasoning using abstract qualitative primitives to encode relations between objects (Cohn and Renz, 2008; Cohn, 1997). One example of such an approach is the Region Connection Calculus (RCC) and its modifications (Chen et al., 2015; Li and Ying, 2004). At the heart of RCC lies the notion of connectedness. Two nonempty regions are connected if and only if their topological closures have a nonempty intersection. Starting with this primitive, one may proceed to define more useful spatial relations such as part-of (x is a part of y if every object that is connected to x is also connected to y) and overlapping (x and y overlap if there is a z that is a part of both x and y). Continuing in the same fashion one can define several other topological notions and then use them to describe spatial configurations objects. While mathematically appealing and facilitating rigorous inference, these qualitative methods are too strict and unable to capture the semantic richness of natural language descriptions of spatial configurations of objects, since they neglect aspects such as orientation, size, shape, and argument types.

It is no surprise that a significant amount of research on locative expressions and spatial relations has been conducted in modern robotics. Using natural language is the most efficient way to issue a command to robots, and since they have to operate in the physical world, understanding the way humans describe space is crucial. Current state-of-the-art approaches to grounding natural language commands in general, and spatial commands in particular, are based on probabilistic graphical models (PGM) such as *Generalized Grounding Graphs* (G^3) (Tellex et al., 2011) and *Distributed Correspondence Graphs* (DCG) (Howard et al., 2014) and their modifications (Broad et al., 2016; Paul et al., 2016; Boteanu et al., 2016; Chung et al., 2015).

Conceptually, the way we define the spatial relations in our model is similar to the *spatial template* approach, discussed in Logan and Sadler (1996). This approach is based on the idea of defining a region of acceptability around the reference object that captures the typical locations of the relatum for this relation and determining how well the actual relatum fits this region. Our work is also similar in spirit and goals to the work by Bigelow et al. (2015), which combined the imagistic space representations with spatial templates and applied it to a story understanding task. In their approach, the authors used explicit graphics modeling of a scene using Blender to represent the objects in question and their relative configurations. In their model, each region of acceptability is a three dimensional rectangular region (more precisely, a prism with a rectangular base) representing the set of points for which the given spatial relation holds. For example if one has a pair of two objects, A and B, and wants to determine whether A is on top of B, A is checked to determine whether it is in the region of acceptability located directly above B. Probabilistic reasoning is supported by using values from 0 to 1 to represent the portion of the relatum that falls into a particular region of acceptability.

In recent years, attempts have been made to use statistical learning models, especially deep neural networks, to learn spatial relations. Noteworthy examples are Bisk et al. (2017) and Chang et al. (2014). The first study was dedicated to learning spatial prepositions from images with accompanying textual annotation data within a blocks world domain. The experimental task was based on a series of images showing step-by-step construction of various structures on a table. Any two consecutive images differed in one block movement, and each image was paired with a textual description of that change. A deep neural architecture was used to pair the spatial descriptions with movements and positions of blocks in the images. The second study in a sense inverted the learning problem; the task was not to learn how to describe object relationships, but rather to automatically generate a scene based on a textual description. As such the work revisits well-studied terrain (Coyne and Sproat, 2001). Another recent study in this area is Yu and Siskind (2017), wherein spatial relation models are used to locate and identify similar objects in several video streams. We should separately mention the spatial modelling studies by Malinowski and Fritz (2014) and, especially, Collell et al. (2017), which apply deep neural networks to learning spatial templates for triplets of form (relatum, relation, referent). The latter work does this in an implicit setting, that is, it uses relations that indirectly suggests certain spatial configurations, e.g., *(person, rides, horse)*. Their model is capable not only of learning a spatial template for specific arguments but also of generalizing that template to previously unseen objects; e.g., it can infer the template for *(person, rides, elephant)*. These approaches, however, rely on the analysis of 2D images rather than attempting to model relations in an explicitly represented 3D world.

3 Proposed Model[1]

Here we describe an example of our models for spatial prepositions as well as some of the underlying concepts and intuitions. The factors that contribute to the semantics of the prepositions can be divided into geometric and non-geometric ones. Geometric factors are relatively straightforward; they include locations, sizes and distances. Non-geometric factors include background knowledge about the relata—their physical properties, roles, the way we interact with them—as well as the perceived "frame" and the presence and characteristics of other objects within that frame.

We use a 3D modeling approach in our work. Thus geometric factors can be directly inferred from the coordinates of the polygonal meshes

---

[1]The implementation and all the accompanying data can be found at https://github.com/gplatono/SRP/tree/master/blender_project

comprising the object's model. We add additional geometric and non-geometric knowledge about the objects by manually attaching labels or tags to the meshes. Our approach is a rule-based one. Each spatial relation takes two (or three, in case of *between*) arguments and applies a sequence of metrics evaluating various criteria, such as distance, whether the objects are in contact, whether they possess certain properties, etc. Each metric returns a real number from $[0, 1]$. Where these metrics represent contributing factors to a relation, they are usually combined linearly into a normalized compound metric, with weights representing the importance of the factors. In some cases two factors are multiplied together, so that each scales the other. For relations with multiple prototypes, the final metric is just the maximum, i.e., we pick the best match.

Whenever possible we rely on approximations to the real 3D meshes of objects, using centroids and bounding boxes (smallest rectangular regions encompassing the objects). There are two main reasons for that. First, we are trying to achieve near real-time performance. Second, in many circumstances, given the object shapes and distances between them, the approximations yield acceptable results. Among the basic geometric primitives used in our models are various distances, scaled by object dimensions, e.g., scaled centroid distance (SCD):

$$SCD(A, B) = \frac{d(Centroid(A), Centroid(B))}{Radius(A) + Radius(B)}.$$

Here d is just the Euclidean distance and *Radius* gives the radius of the sphere, circumscribed around the object. Given two ideally-shaped objects (cubes or spheres) the scaled distance between them will be equal to 1 exactly when they are touching each other. This is a useful measure if the objects are convex or located relatively far apart.

We also introduce similar metrics for certain types of objects that are not compact, i.e., poorly approximated by a sphere. For example, "the chair is near the wall" doesn't mean that the chair is close to the geometric center of the wall. In this case it makes more sense to measure the distance between the center of the chair and the plane of the wall. We use the labels "planar" and "rod" to mark regularly shaped non-compact objects such as walls and pencils, and introduce special distance metrics for these categories. In certain cases, when an object is very irregular or if high precision is required (e.g., when determining if two objects are touching each other) we compute pairwise vertex-to-vertex distances between two meshes.

Another important geometric primitive is an infinite conic region, defined at a vertex by an orientation vector and the angular width of the cone. This primitive is used in computing so-called projective prepositions, such as *above*, etc. This is similar to the idea of an acceptance area in (Bigelow et al., 2015). Also, for prepositions like *to the left/right of*, whose value depends on the observer's vantage point, we project the arguments' meshes onto the observer's visual plane (orthogonal to its frontal or "view" vector) and then work with 2D data, either bounding boxes or entire mesh projections.

One example of non-geometric knowledge that we use is meronymy (part-whole relationships). This knowledge is crucial for dealing with synechdoche, as in "the book is on a bookshelf". In such a case we don't usually mean that the book is directly on the bookshelf (however, this might be the case in certain contexts), but rather that it is located on one the shelves of the bookshelf. Also, knowing about parts is not enough since many real-life objects have multiple parts but we usually interact with just some of them. For example "a magnet on the frigde" will probably be used to designate a situation where the magnet is attached to the fridge's door rather than stuck on the fridge's top surface. Thus, typical interactions affect the salience of different parts and aspects of objects. In our models we mark such salient parts of an object with a special tag.

As noted earlier, the semantics of spatial prepositions does not just depend on their arguments; the perceived frame or scale and the statistics of objects in the vicinity are additional important factors. For some prepositions we first compute the raw value (between 0 and 1) representing the context-independent value of that preposition's metric. That metric is then modified by scaling it up or down depending on the values of this same metric for other objects in the scene. For example, suppose that the raw nearness metric $near\_raw(A, B)$ for two objects A and B is 0.55 out of 1.0. This reflects the fact that without further context, this is an ambiguous situation. However, if B is the closest object to A, i.e.,

$near\_raw(C, A) < 0.55, \forall C(C \neq B)$, we can say that B is *relatively* near A. In this case the final score $near(A, B)$ will be boosted by a small amount (depending on the distribution of the objects in the scene), which will make a more definite judgment possible.

Finally, let's consider the relation *on* as an example, where multiple simple metrics come together. As noted in Example 1, there are many possible configurations that can be described using *on*. Based on these configurations we can discern several stereotypical scenarios, or prototypes, and introduce special rules, each covering one such prototype. For *on* such prototypes include cases where one object is in contact with the upper surface of another; where it is attached to the salient surface of another; where it is part of a group of objects (i.e., stack), such that this whole group is on the second object; etc. We can describe *on* as (partially) depicted in algorithm 1 below.

Algorithm 1 On (The notation $<$3D-vector$>$.z refers to the vertical component)

1: **procedure** ON(A,B)
2:     *on $\leftarrow$ 0.5 * ((Above(A, B) + Touching(A, B))*
3:     **if** $Planar(B)$ and $Larger(B, A)$ and $centroid(A).z > 0.5 * dimensions(A).z$ **then**
4:         $on \leftarrow max(on, Touching(A, B))$
5:         ...
6:     **for** C *in* B **do**
7:         **if** $WorkingPart(C)$ **then**
8:             $on \leftarrow max(on, On(A, C))$
9:     **for** C *in* $Scene \setminus \{A, B\}$ **do**
10:        **if** $On(C, B) > 0.5$ and $\neg Salient(C)$ **then**
11:           $on \leftarrow max(on, 0.95 * On(A, C) * On(C, B))$

As can be seen, we compute *on* by consecutively applying different rules, corresponding to the aforementioned prototypes, and taking the best fit, i.e., the one whose metric has the maximum value. The first rule captures the canonical scenario where an object is directly above another and in contact with it. The next rule applies to situations where an object is in contact with another, bigger, planar object, such as a wall. In addition, the object should be well above the ground, so we require its centroid to be located higher than half of the object's height ($centroid(A).z >$ $0.5 * dimensions(A).z$). We next apply a few more rules covering such standard scenarios. We also check for the possibility of synechdoche by iterating through an object's interactive parts and checking if the relatum can be said to be on one of them. Finally, we check for transitivity: if A is on B and B is on C, then A is likely to be on C. However, the transitivity of *on* is limited. Salient objects break transitivity; e.g., if a book is on the table and the table on the floor, the book cannot be said to be on the floor. (Salience, as used here, is a static, context-independent property of an object.) Also, if there are too many intermediaries between two objects (a book on top of the stack of books, which is, in turn, on the table), the applicability of *on* decreases. This is probably due to the fact that a pile of objects becomes an increasingly salient, composite object the bigger it grows.

4   Testing domains and the annotation effort for spatial prepositions

We now describe the domains in which we tested our models as well as the experimental setup for annotating spatial configurations of objects. The annotated data serve two purposes. First, in order to measure the performance of our rule-based system, in terms of how well it captures the range of meanings of several spatial prepositions, we need to collect actual instances of human spatial judgments. Second, the collected dataset can be used in the future to teach a machine learning model the spatial relations.[2] We chose to study the spatial relations in two domains: a blocks world and a "room world". The first domain consists of a square plane with multiple colored cubical blocks on it, while the second domain represents a typical room interior, containing various everyday items, e.g., furniture, books, food, appliances, etc. The relatively simple blocks world allows us to isolate and investigate the geometric components of the meaning of a particular preposition, while the more complex room domain adds pragmatic considerations to the mix. Both domains are represented as a set of 3D scenes modeled in Blender (Blender Online Community, 2018). 3D models for the scenes were mostly created ad hoc, directly in Blender, using its standard visual modeling tools. The reason behind this is that most pub-

---

[2]However, while our dataset suffices for evaluating our rule-based model, it will require expansion, perhaps via crowdsourcing, for ML purposes

licly available models are designed with different purposes in mind and their part structure in incompatible with our needs. However, several models were borrowed from the public collection of models on Blend Swap (BlendSwap.com, 2018), available under the Creative Commons licence.

(a)

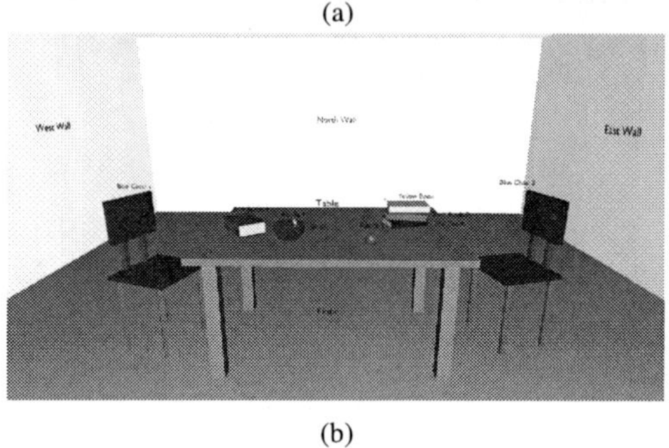

(b)

Figure 1: An example configuration for the the blocks world domain (a) and the room world domain (b)

We set up two different annotation tasks – a truth-judgment task and a description task. In the truth-judgment task, the annotator is presented with a screenshot of a scene from either domain and asked whether the particular relation holds between the given objects ("Is block 1 to the right of block 2?"). The possible qualitative response options form a Likert scale, with five items: "YES", "RATHER YES", "UNCERTAIN", "RATHER NO", "NO". In the description task, the annotator is given a screenshot of a scene from either domain and an object from that scene. The annotator is then asked to describe the object's location, in terms of a single prepositional relation to another object in the scene (or two objects, in exceptional cases like *between* or straddling two objects), so as to identify it uniquely. The annotator is encouraged to provide multiple descriptions, if there are several natural ways to pick out the object uniquely. The list of acceptable prepositions includes the following: *above, below, to the right,*

to the left, in front of, behind, near, at, in, over, under, between, on, and *touching*.[3]

The objects present in the scenes were selected so as to allow for sufficiently varied configurations, combining large immovable items of furniture with multiple portable items. There was no specific plan behind the object placement in any scene, except to ensure that the target object can be uniquely described, and the overall configuration does not look unnatural or anomalous. To make unique descriptive identification of objects nontrivial, some of the objects, such as chairs or books, were presented in the scenes in several identical copies. Annotators were not allowed to directly refer to the objects by their name (every object in the scene was accompanied by a unique identifier to make it easier for the participant to locate it), but, instead, the participants were asked to use only the type and/or color of the objects when referring to them. Examples of acceptable descriptions include "to the left of another black block", "between a table and a bookshelf", "at the bed", and "on two blue blocks". In order to automate the process and facilitate gathering of the dataset, an annotation tool was deployed online and about a dozen volunteers (grad and undergrad students from the computer science department) were asked to participate in the preliminary data collection (Fig. 2). Since the task is straightforward they received minimal training; only the restrictions on the response format (only one preposition, unique identifiability, etc.) were made clear to them.

A number of scenes were created for the proposed annotation tasks. For the description task, 151 scenes were created. For the blocks world, each scene was designed to allow three questions (identification of three different blocks), while the more context-rich room world scenes supported 7-8 questions on average. For the truth-judgment task, 192 scenes were designed, with one question per scene. These 192 scenes are comprised of four variations of 48 basic scenes. The variations are: basic scene (with just the relation argument objects present in the scene), basic scene with bigger frame size (zoomed out), basic scene

---

[3]These particular prepositions were chosen in part because of their naturalness for describing configurations of objects in the original domain (the blocks world) – unlike *across, around, throughout, with, etc.*, and in part by the practical need to limit the number of prepositions to be modeled while still including the most widely used ones.

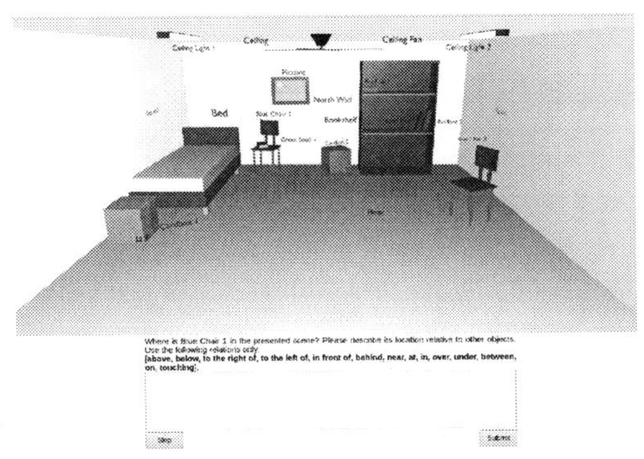

Figure 2: The annotation website. The instructions say "Where is Blue Chair 1 in the presented scene? Please describe its location relative to other objects." The instructions are followed by the list of the fourteen admissible prepositions.

with context (additional objects added), and basic scene with context and bigger frame size. The collected dataset contains approximately 3500 annotations in total, with about 1500 annotations for the truth-judgment task and 2000 for the description task. It was split into a parameter tuning part and a disjoint test set with the latter containing about 800 annotations, split approximately equally between the description and truth-judgment tasks.

5 Evaluation

The model was evaluated as follows. For the truth-judgment task, the model was used to evaluate the given relation and its arguments. Both the numerical answer provided by the model and the annotator's answer were then transformed to the ordinal scale to compute the agreement coefficient. The human responses were converted from the Likert scale "YES", "RATHER YES", "UNCERTAIN", "RATHER NO", "NO" into integers 5 to 1, respectively. The metric value generated by the model was transformed as follows: Values in $[0, 0.2)$ correspond to 1, those in $[0.2, 0.4)$ to 2, ..., those in $[0.8, 1]$ to 5. For the description task, given a human description of a target object in relation to a reference object, the model was given the reference object and relation, and was required to identify the object being described.

We used both standard and weighted versions of Cohen's Kappa as an inter-annotator agreement metric with the weighting penalty $w(i, j) = \|i - j\|$, where i and j are the ordinal conversions of the responses of human annotators and our system.

The agreement values were computed as follows. First, all pairwise agreement values between annotators and between each annotator and the system were computed. Next, the corresponding averages (of human-human and human-system pairs, respectively) were found.

For the initial data set (the part used to some extent to tune the model parameters), the accuracy breakdown was as follows. For weighed Kappa, the average pairwise human-human inter-annotator agreement value was 0.717, whereas the average pairwise system-human agreement metric was 0.682. For standard Kappa, the respective values were 0.536 and 0.479.

For an independent data set used for final evaluation, the values were: human-human agreement, weighted Kappa - 0.76, human-system agreement, weighted Kappa - 0.71, human-human agreement, standard Kappa - 0.52, human-system agreement, standard Kappa - 0.49. Again, all these numbers are pairwise averages. As expected, inter-annotator agreement was not very high.[4] The somewhat lower system-human agreement is still close enough to human-human agreement to indicate the plausibility of our models. Since humans manage to identify referents perfectly well using spatial relations, despite the vagueness of these relations, the key question then was how well our models would do for such usages.

relation	total occurrences	accuracy
to the right of	210	89%
to the left of	212	94%
in front of	118	92%
behind	104	96%
above	81	99%
below	43	98%
over	29	96%
under	135	95%
between	168	93%
at	17	94%
touching	71	93%
near	196	82%
in	31	100%
on	166	90%

Table 1: Fourteen relations, together with the total occurrences within the dataset used for tuning (different annotation) and accuracy per relation.

---

[4]This is not a flaw to be remedied, but simply a reflection of the vagueness of the prepositional relations.

For the description task we computed the accuracy in terms of the percentage of tests with correctly identified objects. The overall system accuracy on the testing data was about 93%; while imperfect, this is an encouraging result. The detailed breakdown for separate relations is provided in Table 1.

relation	total occurrences	accuracy
to the right of	33	88%
to the left of	30	87%
in front of	24	96%
behind	25	92%
above	12	100%
below	11	100%
over	0	0%
under	33	97%
between	37	86%
at	4	100%
touching	30	93%
near	55	93%
in	7	100%
on	75	89%

Table 2: Fourteen relations, together with the total occurrences within the dataset used for final testing (different annotation) and accuracy per relation.

6 Discussion and Conclusion

We considered the problem of designing intuitive computational models of spatial prepositions that combine geometrical information as well as some pieces of commonsense knowledge and contextual information about the arguments. In our experiments in a blocks world and a room world, we achieved reasonable agreement with human "truth" judgments and quite good agreement in a referential description task. We are not aware of other models that achieved this level of success in comparably diverse environments.

All of the existing methods we mentioned have significant limitations; typically they deal adequately with some aspects but fall short on others. The lexical semantics models in linguistics provide the most comprehensive theory of spatial relations as they are used in language. As such they are particularly relevant to natural language processing applications. However, their biggest drawbacks (at least when they attempt to address the polysemy of the prepositions) is that they are hardly formalizable and make reference to large amounts of background knowledge about how people interact with the world. Neither hand-crafting that background knowledge nor learning it automatically from data seems feasible at present. On the other hand, research aimed at precise qualitative spatial models typically puts the emphasis on providing formal frameworks that enable rigorous inference, rather than on approximating human spatial representations and judgments. Unsurprisingly, this bias results in models that are suitable for certain applications, such as navigation and autonomous problem solving, but not for human-machine interaction. A separate problem is that of reconciling qualitative and quantitative spatial models.

Computational approaches popular today mostly rely on learning the meaning of prepositions from data. While they are closer to capturing their natural usage patterns, such models are trained on limited datasets in toy tasks. The generalization capabilities of such models are questionable. In our opinion the path towards comprehensive models of spatial prepositions lies at the intersection of these two major paradigms. The core meanings can be captured by meticulous analysis of the behaviour of the prepositions, while machine learning methods can be applied to adjust the weights of various *a priori* significant factors and ultimately to learn diverse additional pragmatic factors that influence human judgments in context, but are very hard to describe explicitly.

A couple of further insights we gained are worth noting. First, as indicated by the disparity we observed between judgments of truth and identification of referents, experimental design is of utmost importance in this area. Special attention needs to be paid to ensure that the experimental task is natural and sufficiently varied; at the same time, the task should enable isolating the specific meaning aspects of particular prepositions, so that they can be modeled individually. These desiderata are not easily achieved.

Second, physics plays an important role in our understanding of spatial relations. For example, as noted at the outset, *on* is closely connected with the *support* relation; thus, a cable or a rope hanging from the ceiling and touching the table under it will probably not be considered to be on the table. This example breaks the rule-based definition of *on* that we presented above. We did not address the physical aspects of the meaning of spatial prepositions in our work. This deficiency will have to be rectified if our models of spatial prepositions are to correspond more fully to our everyday intuition.

Acknowledgments

This work was supported by DARPA grant W911NF-15-1-0542. We thank our annotation team for their contributions, and the anonymous referees for their very useful comments.

References

Eric Bigelow, Daniel Scarafoni, Lenhart Schubert, and Alex Wilson. 2015. On the need for imagistic modeling in story understanding. *Biologically Inspired Cognitive Architectures*, 11:22–28.

Yonatan Bisk, Kevin J Shih, Yejin Choi, and Daniel Marcu. 2017. Learning interpretable spatial operations in a rich 3d blocks world. *arXiv preprint arXiv:1712.03463*.

Blender Online Community. 2018. *Blender - a 3D modelling and rendering package*. Blender Foundation, Blender Institute, Amsterdam.

BlendSwap.com. 2018. *Blendswap.com*.

Adrian Boteanu, Thomas Howard, Jacob Arkin, and Hadas Kress-Gazit. 2016. A model for verifiable grounding and execution of complex natural language instructions. In *Intelligent Robots and Systems (IROS), 2016 IEEE/RSJ International Conference on*, pages 2649–2654. IEEE.

Alexander Broad, Jacob Arkin, Nathan Ratliff, Thomas Howard, Brenna Argall, and Distributed Correspondence Graph. 2016. Towards real-time natural language corrections for assistive robots. In *RSS Workshop on Model Learning for Human-Robot Communication*.

Angel Chang, Manolis Savva, and Christopher D Manning. 2014. Learning spatial knowledge for text to 3d scene generation. In *Proceedings of the 2014 Conference on Empirical Methods in Natural Language Processing (EMNLP)*, pages 2028–2038.

Juan Chen, Anthony G Cohn, Dayou Liu, Shengsheng Wang, Jihong Ouyang, and Qiangyuan Yu. 2015. A survey of qualitative spatial representations. *The Knowledge Engineering Review*, 30(01):106–136.

Istvan Chung, Oron Propp, Matthew R Walter, and Thomas M Howard. 2015. On the performance of hierarchical distributed correspondence graphs for efficient symbol grounding of robot instructions. In *Intelligent Robots and Systems (IROS), 2015 IEEE/RSJ International Conference on*, pages 5247–5252. IEEE.

Anthony G Cohn. 1997. Qualitative spatial representation and reasoning techniques. In *KI-97: Advances in Artificial Intelligence*, pages 1–30. Springer.

Anthony G Cohn and Jochen Renz. 2008. Qualitative spatial representation and reasoning. *Handbook of knowledge representation*, 3:551–596.

Guillem Collell, Luc Van Gool, and Marie-Francine Moens. 2017. Acquiring common sense spatial knowledge through implicit spatial templates. *arXiv preprint arXiv:1711.06821*.

Gloria S Cooper. 1968. A semantic analysis of english locative prepositions. Technical report, DTIC Document.

Bob Coyne and Richard Sproat. 2001. Wordseye: an automatic text-to-scene conversion system. In *Proceedings of the 28th annual conference on Computer graphics and interactive techniques*, pages 487–496. ACM.

Annette Herskovits. 1985. Semantics and pragmatics of locative expressions. *Cognitive Science*, 9(3):341–378.

Thomas M Howard, Stefanie Tellex, and Nicholas Roy. 2014. A natural language planner interface for mobile manipulators. In *Robotics and Automation (ICRA), 2014 IEEE International Conference on*, pages 6652–6659. IEEE.

Alice Kyburg. 2000. When vague sentences inform: a model of assertability. *Synthese*, 124:175–191.

Daniel Lassiter and Noah D. Goodman. 2017. Adjectival vagueness in a Bayesian model of interpretation. *Synthese*, 194:3801–3836.

Sanjiang Li and Mingsheng Ying. 2004. Generalized region connection calculus. *Artificial Intelligence*, 160(1):1–34.

Gordon D Logan and Daniel D Sadler. 1996. A computational analysis of the apprehension of spatial relations. *Language and space*.

Mateusz Malinowski and Mario Fritz. 2014. A pooling approach to modelling spatial relations for image retrieval and annotation. *arXiv preprint arXiv:1411.5190*.

R Paul, J Arkin, N Roy, and TM Howard. 2016. Efficient grounding of abstract spatial concepts for natural language interaction with robot manipulators. *Proceedings of Robotics: Science and Systems (RSS), Ann Arbor, Michigan, USA*.

Stefanie Tellex, Thomas Kollar, Steven Dickerson, Matthew R Walter, Ashis Gopal Banerjee, Seth J Teller, and Nicholas Roy. 2011. Understanding natural language commands for robotic navigation and mobile manipulation. In *AAAI*, volume 1, page 2.

Andrea Tyler and Vyvyan Evans. 2003. *The semantics of English prepositions: Spatial scenes, embodied meaning, and cognition.* Cambridge University Press.

Haonan Yu and Jeffrey Mark Siskind. 2017. Sentence directed video object codiscovery. *International Journal of Computer Vision*, 124(3):312–334.

Lexical Conceptual Structure of Literal and Metaphorical Spatial Language: A Case Study of *Push*

Bonnie Dorr
Institute for Human and Machine Cognition
15 SE Osceola Ave
Ocala, FL 34471
bdorr@ihmc.us

Mari Broman Olsen
Microsoft Natural Language Experiences
One Microsoft Way
Redmond, WA 98052
molsen@microsoft.com

Abstract

Prior methodologies for understanding spatial language have treated literal expressions such as *Mary pushed the car over the edge* differently from metaphorical extensions such as *Mary's job pushed her over the edge*. We demonstrate a methodology for standardizing literal and metaphorical meanings, by building on work in Lexical Conceptual Structure (LCS), a general-purpose representational component used in machine translation. We argue that spatial predicates naturally extend into other fields (e.g., circumstantial or temporal), and that LCS provides both a framework for distinguishing spatial from non-spatial, and a system for finding metaphorical meaning extensions. We start with MetaNet (MN), a large repository of conceptual metaphors, condensing 197 spatial entries into sixteen top-level categories of motion frames. Using naturally occurring instances of English *push*, and expansions of MN frames, we demonstrate that literal and metaphorical extensions exhibit patterns predicted and represented by the LCS model.

1 Introduction

This paper explores representation and distribution of spatial metaphoric language, by identifying instances from the MetaNet (MN) repository of metaphors (David and Lakoff, 2013; Dodge et al., 2015; Stickles et al., 2015), clustering them according to common expressions (e.g., "change of location"), and representing both the literal and metaphorical senses of these expressions as combinations of primitives from Lexical Conceptual Structure (LCS) (Jackendoff, 1983, 1990; Dorr, 1993; Dowty, 1979; Guerssel et al., 1985).

We leverage the *LCS Verb Database* (Dorr et al., 2001), taking LCS as the underlying spatial language meaning representation for literal senses, and aligning these with representations for their corresponding metaphorical representations. For

example, the expression *push over the edge* has a literal (spatial) MN sense, "change of location," that is represented as *CAUSE GO Loc* in the LCS, but its metaphorical MN sense, "change of state," is represented as *CAUSE GO Ident*. As an illustration of this contrast, the expanded LCS representations that include these primitive combinations are shown below:

- Literal (spatial): Mary pushed the car over the edge
```
[Cause MARY
  [Go Loc CAR
    [Toward Over <location>]]],
  <location>=EDGE]
```
- Figurative (metaphorical): Mary's job pushed her over the edge
```
[Cause JOB
  [Go Ident MARY
    [Toward At <result(property)>]]],
  <result(property)>=CRAZY]
```

The focus here is not on the processes necessary for distinguishing between literal and metaphorical senses, but rather on the representational formalism and organizing principles underlying both. The intention is to lay the foundation for subsequent application of additional context and higher order processes for disambiguation, such as visual grounding (Wilks, 1995) or beliefs and inference (Ballim et al., 2007). The main lesson of this study is that there are similarities between the literal and metaphorical expressions, and that these can be seen through analysis into LCS primitives without extra visual/reasoning evidence.

As a starting point for exploring metaphoric language, 197 spatially grounded metaphors were identified in MN from the total collection of 684 MN entries. These were organized into a smaller set of classes (139) through automatic identification of duplicated phrases (e.g.,"change of location"), and then further reduced to 16 classes of metaphorical LCS representations, paired with

Proceedings of the First International Workshop on Spatial Language Understanding (SpLU-2018), pages 31–40
New Orleans, Louisiana, June 6, 2018. ©2018 Association for Computational Linguistics

their corresponding spatially grounded counterparts in the Loc(ational) field.

To explore the diversity in naturally occurring texts, we used a corpus of around 30k Word documents from the Microsoft language resource library, and available for research. The documents had been harvested from an approved index of websites (excluding sites that are copyrighted, marked do not crawl, adult content, and other restrictions)[1] and targeted specific English locale settings,[2] as represented by properties of the file format.

An initial search with text processing tools for Windows (public and proprietary) yielded more than 10k en-us sentences for the following spatial and motion strings: *extend, span, contain, come, go, push, pull, enter, exit, rise, fall, skyrocket, plummet, turn back, forge ahead, headway, get out of, get into, drive, be down, be up, be in, be out, guide, follow, sprint, creep, drain, move along, advance.* We scoped this to just under 2k "*Push* Sentences" – small enough to review, but large enough to present an interesting distribution of forms.

The availability of these two resources enabled the systematic division into LCS classes based on common pairs, and the exploration of naturally occurring instances of them, without requiring a large-scale manual annotation effort. The 16 resulting LCS classes correspond to groupings based on common pairs of metaphorical and spatial LCS's, as extracted from the LCS Verb Database, as in the example above: *CAUSE GO Loc* (literal) ↔ *CAUSE BE Ident* (metaphorical).

Examples of derived classes are shown here:

- **Class 1 (Being at a Location)**

    - Spatial/Literal: The ice *pushed away* from the Arctic and into the Atlantic (GO LOC TOWARD).
    - Metaphorical: My mind *pushed away* all the frustration (GO IDENT STATE)

- **Class 4 (Manner of Motion)**

    - Spatial/Literal: The woman *pushed aside* the book and fell asleep (CAUSE GO LOC MANNER)

    - Metaphorical: The team should *push aside* thoughts of failure (CAUSE GO PERC MANNER)

- **Class 5 (Movement along a path)**

    - Spatial/Literal: Mary *pushed* the car *over* the edge (CAUSE GO LOC PATH)
    - Metaphorical: Mary's job *pushed* her *over* the edge (CAUSE GO IDENT STATE)

We used the *Push* Sentences to examine these derived classes systematically, analyzing their spatial/metaphorical distribution, as well as the coverage of the spatially based derived metaphor classes. This systematic comparison identified missing metaphor entries in MN, as well as metaphorical instances of *push* not occurring in the corpus, that we found attested in a general web search of the pattern.

The pairing of MN entries with their LCS representations has enabled identification and representation of literal/metaphorical pairs that can be used for downstream natural language understanding. Our corpus-based research both supports the derived classes, and suggests expansion of them. This treatment of both literal and metaphorical extensions of the predicates also provides a framework for a structured search of both possible gaps in the metaphor inventory, and possible metaphoric extensions of individual predicates.

Prior work (Jackendoff, 1996; Levin, 1993; Olsen, 1994; Kipper et al., 2007; Palmer et al., 2017) has suggested that there is a close relation between underlying lexical-semantic structures of predicates and their syntactic argument structure. It has been claimed that prepositional argument constraints on motion predicates need not distinguish between literal and metaphorical senses (Chang et al., 2007, 2010). We take this earlier work a step further by examining generalizations of systematicity at the syntax-semantics interface between literal and metaphorical senses of spatial and motion predicates.

Section 2 provides background on metaphor and how it has been represented, generally and for computational applications. We introduce the LCS representation and MN resource, and describe how we extracted spatial metaphors from the latter and represented them by the former. We illustrate the work with an excerpt of a table provided in the supplemental material. Sec-

---

[1]Nevertheless we may not share the extracted sentence corpus without seeking permission from the document authors. We do not think this negates the conclusions of this paper, as the corpus is referential, and the examples not unusual.

[2]English locales include US, Australia, Canada, New Zealand, Great Britain, and others.

tion 3 describes the mapping of spatial metaphors to LCS. Section 4 discusses the *Push* Sentences. We show how to represent *push* metaphors in LCS according to the derived spatial metaphor classes, extend the classes to address cases of *push* absent from MN examples, and the converse: examples predicted to occur that were absent from the corpus. We conclude that the richness of the syntactic patterns available to Spatial (literal) uses of verbs and related nominals are also available to their metaphorical counterparts, thus providing a structured way to investigate and represent metaphorical data, including future work exploring whether and why distributional differences may occur. In Section 5 we discuss related work (Cascades (David et al., 2016)) and future explorations (multilingual representation, for which LCS was originally designed).

2   Background

Lexical Conceptual Structure (LCS) (Jackendoff, 1983, 1990; Dorr, 1993; Dowty, 1979; Guerssel et al., 1985) has been used for a range of different applications, including interlingual machine translation (Habash and Dorr, 2002), lexical acquisition (Habash et al., 2006), cross-language information retrieval (Levow et al., 2000), language generation (Traum and Habash, 2000), and intelligent language tutoring (Dorr, 1997).

LCS primitives are defined so that their combination captures syntactic generalities: actions and entities must be systematically related to a syntactic structure. Constraints operate on three dimensions: (1) spatial, (2) causal, and (3) field. The primitive building blocks include GO, STAY, BE, GO-EXT, ORIENT, and also an ACT primitive developed by Dorr and Olsen, (1997). These primitives come from the spatial dimension and have the following syntactic and semantic argument selection constraints:

Events (Argument1, Argument2):
  GO(Thing, Path) *Jen ran home*
  STAY(Thing, Position) *Jen remained home*
  ACT(Thing, Thing) *Jen ate dinner*
States (Argument1, Argument2):
  BE(Thing, Position) *Jen was home*
  ORIENT(Thing, Path) *The sign points to the exit*
  GO-EXT(Thing, Path) *The highway runs through Montana*

In the Causal dimension, predicates CAUSE and LET have two arguments: a Thing or Event,

and a State or Event. The Field dimension describes Argument relations as:
  (Loc)ational (pertaining to space/motion)
  (Poss)essional (ownership)
  (Temp)oral (time)
  (Ident)ificational (state)
  (Circ)umstantial (situation)
  (Exist)ential (existence)
  (Perc)eptual (perception)
  (Comm)unicational (communication)

The latter two fields (Perceptual and Communicational) correspond to two domains added by Olsen et al. (1997) beyond the original LCS conceptualization of Jackendoff (1983; 1990), enabling coverage of a wider range of metaphorical extensions.

Within the LCS framework, both literal (spatial) and figurative (metaphorical) meanings are captured for a wide range of verbal constructions. The spatial dimension of the LCS representation (i.e., the *(Loc)ational* field) serves as the basis of the *literal* meaning, thus enabling straightforward extension to the other fields to represent the *metaphorical* meaning. This extension supports a systematic mapping of spatial meaning to surface realizations. This systematicity correspondingly carries over to metaphorical counterparts and a systematic surface realization is available for both types of meanings.

For example, the GO primitive in the Loc field projects a prepositional phrase containing a location, such as *over the edge*, whereas the GO primitive in the Ident field projects an adjectival phrase containing a property, such as *crazy*. Additional examples of the three dimensions above are discussed in Section 3.

This paradigm is consistent with that of Neuman et al., (2013) in large-scale metaphor identification, which takes meanings of the word as literal (or non-metaphorical) based on "how close the word's sense is to its embodied origins," vs. determining the same by frequency, commonsense, or selectional preference strategies.[3]

Representations of spatial relations and their metaphorical extensions to other domains have been the subject of numerous studies (Talmy, 1985; Gentner, 2001). The benefit of this LCS-based grounding of metaphorical expressions in their spatial counterparts is that it is possible to leverage a set of principled mappings from LCS to

---

[3]Even so they acknowledge that identifying metaphors is difficult even for humans.

33

Class 1: Be at Location (MN: EXPERIENCED STATE IS PROXIMATE OBJECT)	
Examples: *...a headache approaching* (MN); *...migraine **pushed** itself through skull* (Push Sentences)	
Spatial/Literal:	**Metaphorical:**
LCS: go loc [state] toward y	LCS: go ident y toward [state]
RED: GO LOC TOWARD	RED: GO IDENT STATE
Class 4: Manner of Motion (MN: GUIDED ACTION IS GUIDED MOTION ALONG PATH)	
Examples: *...guided through the task* (MN); *...**pushed** products to marketplace* (Push Sentences)	
Spatial/Literal:	**Metaphorical:**
LCS: cause x go loc y toward z [manner]	LCS: cause x go perc y toward z [manner]
RED: CAUSE GO LOC MANNER	RED: CAUSE GO PERC MANNER
Class 5: Change of Location (MN: CHANGE OF STATE IS CHANGE OF LOCATION)	
Examples: *...fell into depression* (MN); *...**pushed** her over the edge* (Push Sentences)	
Spatial/Literal:	**Metaphorical:**
LCS: cause x go loc toward y [location]	LCS: cause x go ident y toward [state]
RED: CAUSE GO LOC PATH	RED: CAUSE GO IDENT STATE

Table 1: Sample of LCS-Based Classification for Literal (Spatial) and Metaphorical Senses with Examples from MN and 'Push' Sentences

syntactic realizations for a wide range of verb semantics within 192 verb classes of (Levin, 1993), augmented by 44 additional classes that were subsequently added (Dorr, 1997) and further enhanced for aspectual composition (Olsen, 1994; Dorr and Olsen, 1997; Dorr et al., 2001).

For a rich source of metaphoric constructions, we leveraged MetaNet (MN), a repository of metaphors represented in accordance with principles of conceptual metaphor theory, introduced by Lakoff and Johnson (1980). The metaphors each map a Source domain (e.g. "life") to a Target domain (e.g. "journey"), yielding metaphors like *Life is a journey*.

Both Source and Target domains are themselves represented as rich conceptual frames in MN. For example, *someone* lives a life, with a *span*, possibly with a *companion*, and a *goal*, etc. These map to elements of the 'journey' frame as, respectively, *journey-er*, the *journey* event and *companion*, and the *destination*.

Additional MN mappings in the network of concepts include stops, paths, locations along the way, vehicles, etc. Examples of surface realizations are also included with the metaphor, e.g. *His life has taken a good course* and *He has changed his direction in life, and taken a more spiritual path.* (Neuman et al., 2018; David and Lakoff, 2013; Dodge et al., 2015; Stickles et al., 2015)

In addition, frames can be linked to frames, and metaphors to metaphors, defining larger networks. For example, "CAUSED CHANGE OF STATE" *is subcase of* "CAUSATION", and *makes use of* "CHANGE OF STATE" (Neuman et al., 2018).

We look at metaphors comprised of a mapping between a concept for a literal expression typi-cally related to space or motion like "CHANGE OF LOCATION," and the corresponding concept for the metaphorical sense, e.g., "CHANGE OF STATE." So, for example, the surface realization *pushed him over the edge* is an (adapted) example associated with a mapping between the literal meaning of *push* (CHANGE OF LOCATION) and the metaphorical meaning of *push* (CHANGE OF STATE) which, in this case, could be paraphrased as *go crazy*.

3 Spatial Language Metaphors: Mapping to Lexical Semantic Representations

Understanding how spatial expressions relate to objects and situations in the real world can enable an understanding of abstract notions that "inherit" properties of their spatial analogues. Even without the context of a visual stream (Wilks, 1995) or access to beliefs and inferential processes (Ballim et al., 2007), it is possible to support sentence-processing applications (e.g., grammar checking) by relying on a lexical-semantic representation that enables uniform syntactic analysis, within a framework that supports downstream processing for disambiguation.

We conducted an analysis of the MN metaphor repository, identifying 197 spatially grounded metaphors and collapsing these into 139 unique spatial expressions. We then categorized these into 16 semantically motivated classes based on pairings between LCS primitives for the spatial/literal sense and LCS primitives for the metaphorical sense. Table 1 shows representative spatial and metaphorical cases for the three derived classes introduced in Section 1, together with examples

Class Name	Spatial/Literal	Metaphorical	Examples	PUSH EXAMPLE
1. (Being at) Location / Position /	be loc x not_at y [REDUCED: BE LOC NOT_AT]	be exist x not_at [exist] [REDUCED: BE EXIST NOT_AT]	He's gone/departed	~He's pushed off [=left]
	go loc [state] toward y [REDUCED: GO LOC TOWARD]	(1) go ident y toward [state<property>] [REDUCED: GO IDENT STATE] (2) be poss y at [state<condition>] [REDUCED: BE POSS STATE]	I feel /a head ache approaching/	~[headache] feels like a creature pushing itself through my skull
2. Force Acting on Motion	cause x go loc y toward [event] [REDUCED: CAUSE GO LOC TOWARD]	(1) cause x go ident y toward [event<property>] [REDUCED: CAUSE GO IDENT STATE] (2) cause x go circ y toward [event<partnership>] [REDUCED: CAUSE GO CIRC EVENT]	Her parents pushed her into marriage	~parents pushed her into marriage ~[project] helped pushing forward industry structure adjustment ~pushed to détente ~pushed our country into the muck of depravity
	cause x go loc y toward z [REDUCED: CAUSE GO LOC TOWARD]	cause x go exist y toward [exist] [REDUCED: CAUSE GO EXIST TOWARD]	Democrats pushed through historic legislation	~A coalition group ... [is] trying to push along the referendum ~Hollywood media moguls are pushing an agenda ~a delegation to push against delays and ... taxes
	cause x go loc y toward z [manner] [REDUCED: CAUSE GO LOC MANNER]	act_on x y [result_of_manner_toward_z] [REDUCED: ACT_ON RESULT_OF_MANNER_TOWARD]	They drove the country into a ditch	~help push downtown [business area] to upgrade
3. (Change of) Possession	cause x stay loc [state] at x [REDUCED: CAUSE STAY LOC STATE]	cause x stay poss x at [state] [REDUCED: CAUSE STAY POSS STATE]	The president kept hold of power	~youth who have been pushed out of their homes
	cause x go loc y away_from z [REDUCED: CAUSE GO LOC AWAY_FROM]	cause x go poss y away_from z [REDUCED: CAUSE GO POSS AWAY_FROM]	Radicals seized control of the city from the ruling party	~control these thoughts, or push them out of your mind
4. Manner of Motion	cause x go loc y toward z [manner] [REDUCED: CAUSE GO LOC MANNER]	cause x go perc y toward z [manner] [REDUCED: CAUSE GO PERC MANNER]	She guided him through the problem	~push yourself to places you have never been before
	go loc x toward y [manner] [REDUCED: GO LOC MANNER]	go perc x toward y [manner] [REDUCED: GO PERC MANNER]	We slogged through it	~pushed products into the marketplace ~push students past their current language level
	act loc x along y [manner] [REDUCED: ACT LOC ALONG MANNER]	go circ x toward y [result_of_manner_on_y] [REDUCED: GO CIRC RESULT_OF_MANNER]	We will smoothly sail along for the rest of the process	~pushing down decision making to lower levels ~a group needs to be pushed forward or a path to follow.
	cause x go loc x [path] z [REDUCED: CAUSE GO LOC PATH]	go circ x toward z [REDUCED: GO CIRC TOWARD]	She successfully navigated her way through negotiations	~push your brother out for his walk

Table 2: Excerpt of Derived Classes for Literal (Spatial) and Metaphorical Senses with MN and 'Push' Examples

from MN and Push Sentences. Each class has one of 16 labels (e.g., "Be at Location" or "Manner of Motion"). A single MN entry is shown in the table for each class, e.g., "EXPERIENCED STATE IS PROXIMATE OBJECT", although, in general, each class may be associated with multiple MN entries.

In each class, an LCS representation is provided for the **Spatial/Literal** sense and another LCS is provided for the **Metaphorical** sense. These LCS's are indexed by a set of "reduced" primitives (RED), such as "GO LOC TOWARD," that represent the salient components of the full LCS. The coupling of the reduced primitives for the literal sense with those of the metaphorical sense are what enabled the development of each of the 16 classes. For example, the "Be at Location" class emerged from the coupling of "GO LOC TOWARD" with "GO IDENT STATE," as well as additional couplings that are further fleshed out in a supplemental resource described in Section A. The 16 derived classes were named once they emerged from these couplings.

It is interesting to note that the three Push examples in Table 1 (one per each of Class 1, 4, and 5) were not available in MN, but were mined from the *Push* Sentences. Out of all 16 classes, only Class 2 (Force Acting on Motion) contained MN sentences with the word *push*. These were in fact the only sentences in the entire MN inventory that contained the word *push*:

- ...her parents kept **push**ing her [into an arranged marriage][4]
- ...Democrats **push** through historic, controversial healthcare legislation[5]
- ...Bloomberg goes to Washington to **push** gun laws[6]

As such, this study has revealed several cases of Metaphors containing the word *push* that were not found in MN, but were systematically identified and accordingly classified. More specifically, with the exception of the derived classes 7, 8, and 13, examples were extracted anew from *Push* Sentences and assigned to the appropriate derived classes per LCS-based predictions (e.g., *migraine pushed itself through her skull*).[7] We therefore systematize the MN representation of Space/Motion and extend its coverage. Coupled with the LCS Verb Database this extended MN provides a framework for future research in English and other languages.

---

[4]from MN entry "CAUSED CHANGE OF STATE IS CAUSED CHANGE OF LOCATION"

[5]from MN entry "ENACTING LEGISLATION IS CAUSING MOTION ALONG A PATH"

[6]from MN entry "INCITING GOVERNING ACTION IS FORCED MOVEMENT"

[7]For Classes 7, 8, and 13, no example was found in the *Push* sentences.

Table 2 shows an excerpt of a table provided in the supplemental material. The first column provides the name of the newly emerged class from this study. The next two columns contain the LCS's and corresponding reduced primitives for the Literal (Spatial) and Metaphorical senses, respectively. The "Examples" column contains examples from MN. The "PUSH EXAMPLE" column contains additional metaphorical expressions extracted from the *Push* Sentences—a representative sample of the total number of 1655 sentences containing the word *push*. The supplemental material also includes hyperlinked MN entries for each example associated with each class, enabling the addition of new metaphors to MN.

Note that metaphorical extensions of spatial notions such as *up, down, into, from, to, over* to abstract notions in MN such as *go crazy, become depressed, feel badly* can enable realizations of metaphorical expressions that mirror those of their literal (spatial) counterparts. Motion frames are systematically realized in language with motion syntax. Metaphorical extensions of spatial language analogously would similarly permit a variety of motion expression forms.

This observation has been leveraged for natural language analysis in writing assistance applications (Chang et al., 2007, 2010), relying on the subcategorization frame parallels in literal and metaphoric language. For example, consider the derived Manner of Motion class 4 (*guide, lead, launch, shove, roll, walk, run, climb, hike,...*). Verbs in this class describe translational motion of a particular type, in the spatial (literal) meaning. In the spatial domain, these verbs may also have complements that signify the PATH of the motion, as well as the beginning and ending points of the Path (SOURCE, GOAL). If the motion is self-propelled, the verbs appear in intransitive constructions[8] with various verb-phrase arguments expressing the beginning, extent, and end of the motion:

- We're running.
- We're walking on the Burke-Gilman Trail.
- We're rolling on the Burke-Gilman Trail from Golden Gardens Park.
- We're hiking to the Ballard Locks on the Burke-Gilman Trail.

Similarly, verbs like *push/pull* inherently encode an exertion of force,[9] patterning like motion verbs with all the predicted complements (generally appearing transitively).

- We're pushing (the stroller).
- We're pushing the stroller on the trail
- We're pushing the stroller on the trail from the park.
- We're pushing the stroller to the locks from the park.

Additionally, these verbs can have temporal adjuncts, e.g. *on Tuesday, this summer*. Therefore we expect (and see) a wide variety of prepositional phrases associated with verbs, and natural language understanding needs to be appropriately constrained. Chang et al. (2007; 2010) observed that complements of motion verbs appeared in the same constructions, whether the meanings were literal or metaphorical, and therefore attachment in parsing of prepositional phrases could be guided by similar constraints, permitting (but not requiring) a beginning, extent, and end of the motion.

- He's just walking through life. [PATH]
- We're running the conference from Friday, June 1, through weekend, to Monday June 4.
- The responsibility drove her over the edge.
- We're pushing the meeting back to next Friday.

In the *Push* Sentences we see similar variety in the derived classes that employ these verbs. For example, *Push your way through finals* is understood by metaphorical extension of spatially-related motion examples such as *Push your way through the crowd*. More generally, organizing metaphors into LCS-based classes enables the prediction of possible syntactic realizations on the surface.

An important contribution of this work derives from the LCS-based organizational structure, which enables enrichment and expansion of MN, as discussed further in Section 5.

4 Case Study: push

Prior work (Chang et al., 2007, 2010) was designed to enable writing assistance (e.g. grammar

---

[8](Levin, 1993)'s class of *Roll Verbs* has finer-grained classifications.

[9](Levin, 1993)'s *Verbs of Exerting Force*

Part of Speech	Spatial	Metaphorical	Unknown
Verbs: 998	46% (459)	52% (514)	2% (25)
Nouns: 637	70.6% (450)	26.5% (169)	2.8% (18)
Adjectives: 20	45% (9)	55% (11)	(0)

Table 3: Summary of Spatial and Metaphorical Usages for *push* in 1655 sentences/lines of the Corpus

Noun type	Spatial	Metaphorical	Unknown
Simple: 118	36.4% (43)	54.2% (64)	9.3% (11)
Agentive: 7	0% (0)	57% (4)	43% (3)
Compound: 512	79.3% (406)	18.5% (100)	1.2% (6)

Table 4: Noun Spatial and Metaphorical Usages for *push* by Subtype

checking) as an application for deep understanding of lexical conceptual structure, including directional and spatial language. This earlier work proposed that spatial expressions enable structural realizations across both literal and metaphorical usages across languages, with examples from English, Spanish, German, French, and Japanese. In this section we illustrate the validity of this assumption for spatial expressions involving *push*, exploring both spatial and metaphorical usages derived from the *Push* Sentences.

In our analysis, we found that 52% of the verb occurrences of in the *Push* Sentences were used in their metaphorical sense. So, although only 28% of metaphors in MN had spatial origins, spatial expressions involving *push* were prevalent in the form of metaphorical extensions and, moreover, even in these extended senses adhered to syntactic structures and complements of their spatial counterparts. Therefore, it is important to capture the cross-field units of meaning (something akin to *exert force against some form of resistance*) while also supporting predictable cross-field surface realizations.

After discarding 71 instances from the 1726 sentences with the string *push* as irrelevant (lines of code, *Pushkin*, etc.), we categorized the remaining 1655 instances by part of speech, and identified, context permitting, whether the use was spatial or metaphorical.

The results in Table 3 show almost 40% of the uses across parts of speech were metaphorical, with 52% of the 998 Verbs and 55% of the Adjectives (20). Of the 998 verbs, the metaphorical uses included technical terms (*push notifications (to someone)*), political advocacy (*e.g. push legislation, a referendum, an agenda*),[10] marketing (*push a brand, Christmas specials*), and motivation (*push into college, push through AP classes*). Spatial uses included *push a button/laundry cart/box*. Sentences with Unknown verb uses did not provide enough context to identify whether they referred to spatial or metaphorical *pushing*, for example (*you push through and nature sings; always push and do not pull, the work done in pushing back the atmosphere*).

We note, in particular, that both the verbal and nominal uses exhibit similar syntactic structures to **both** the literal (spatial) and figurative (metaphorical) usages. For example, as shown in Table 4, the 637 nouns included simple spatial/metaphorical examples terms (*a push into college/the door*) and metaphorical agentives (*drug/token/domino pusher*).[11] Compounds included spatial phrases (*push button, push-button, pushbutton, push/pull handle, pushpin, push-ups, push piers*) and metaphorical phrases (*push factor, push-notification, push web services, push promotion strategies, push-in class services, push subscription*).[12,13]

In LCS, these would be treated as conflational variants or divergences (Dorr, 1993). The nominal would express a conflated EVENT that could be the subject of a predicate, for example *A **push** into college gave Mary her start.*

Finally, we discovered that *push* can appear in most spatial/motion metaphor categories, as indicated in italicized examples inserted into Table 2, and also into supplemental material. We show examples in English, and suggest meanings that may not be idiomatic in English, but could be predicted in other languages (e.g. based on fields). In each of these cases, the meaning of *push* was consistent with its role as a verb of exerting force, potentially causing motion. With the addition of these examples, it is clear that our LCS-based structuring of MN has allowed us to systematically predict and find Metaphors not found in MN.

We do not claim that the categorization is ready to be standardized, or that the distribution is representative—be it across texts, across spatial/motion predicates, across languages for verbs meaning 'push', of all the metaphors involving

---

[10]See (David et al., 2016) for extensive discussion of advocacy pertaining to *gun rights*.

[11]The other examples *toolpusher, pedal pusher* cannot be analyzed with confidence given the short contexts.

[12]Unknown again had limited context, e.g. *"short response plyo push-up."*

[13]Hyphenated, closed, and open compounds were included in each case.

'push' in English, or in any other way. We offer the numbers and text examples[14] as qualitative evidence of the breadth and variety of metaphorical extensions in naturally occurring texts.

5 Discussion and Future Work

The work presented in this paper is complementary to, and not incompatible with, downstream visual grounding for disambiguation (Wilks, 1995) or belief ascription for metaphor identification (Ballim et al., 2007). The LCS framework aims to provide a systematic mapping to surface realizations, without requiring disambiguation, but still enabling further distinctions to be made between literal and metaphorical meanings through additional context such as visual inputs or higher order beliefs and reasoning and others, including selectional restrictions and word embeddings (Dinh and Gurevych, 2016).

Collapsing the spatially-motivated metaphors into semantic classes is similar to the Cascade approach (David et al., 2016) that uses the MN foundation as a starting point. Both LCS and Cascades provide a framework within which to bring order to the collection of observations: hierarchical concepts in the case of Cascades and lexical-conceptual structure in the case of the framework described in this paper. The lexical conceptual structure focuses on how the semantics of literal and metaphorical verbs projects into syntax, whereas Cascades describe how the semantics of individual metaphors organize hierarchically, and how they relate to grammatical constructions.

The LCS framework offers consistent structure across literal and metaphoric domains within and between languages. It may be that the variation we see in *which* lexical elements are used in languages can be attributed to the different perspectives on the events they name, similar to the particulars in the two perspectives on gun rights. For example, are there meaningful differences in the use of *push* in English, mirroring Spanish uses of *promover, impulsar, inculcar, esforzar* in Table 5?

The Cascades approach suggests there is a continuum from literal to metaphorical—that the dividing line is not clear. Our data analysis of spatially motivated metaphors revealed the validity of this continuum. This suggests future research on adding a continuous dimension beyond what

E:	The NRA pushed the pro-gun legislation (through congress).
S:	La NRA **promovió / impulsó** la legislación pro-armas (en el congreso).
E:	My parents **pushed** me to succeed.
S:	Mis padres me **inculcaron** el tratar de ser exitoso.
E:	I **pushed** myself through my AP classes.
S:	Me **esforcé** mucho con las clases avanzadas.
E:	The ice cream shop pushed peppermint for the holidays. (as in encouraged sales).
S:	La heladería **promovió / intentó / colocó / insistió mucho** con el helado de menta en las fiestas.

Table 5: Spanish Usages of English *push*

is provided in the LCS framework. For example, when one army pushes another back to a position, or the US pushes the indigenous peoples to a reservation, there is no contact involved, but the pushing seems more direct (and probably would involve contact if challenged) than pushing someone over the (metaphorical) edge or pushing a bill through congress.

Another promising avenue for future research would be the identification of multilingual equivalents of the 139 unique spatial expressions that were extracted from MN in this study. Such an endeavor would involve the construction of analogous representations of these 139 cases for other languages–thus enabling a cross-lingual mapping that would yield potential metaphorical extensions. Testing these metaphorical extensions would proceed in each language by examining cross-field analogues, as in the English case. Ultimately, it would be critical to demonstrate the multilingual relevance of this representational mapping for processes such as PP attachment.

Acknowledgments

We would like to acknowledge and thank three anonymous reviewers for their careful reading of our manuscript and their many insightful comments and constructive suggestions. The first author is supported, in part, by the Institute for Human and Machine Cognition. The second author is supported, in part, by Microsoft.

References

Afzal Ballim, Yorick Wilks, and John Barnden. 2007. Belief Ascription, metaphor, and Intensional Identification. *Words and Intelligence I: text, Speech and Language technology* 35:217–253.

Su Chin Chang, Ravi C. Shahani, Domenic J. Cipollone, Michael V. Calcagno, Mari J. B. Olsen, and David J. Parkinson. 2007. Linguistic Object

---

[14]Examples have been truncated or otherwise adapted in accordance with Microsoft company policy

Model. 7,171,352. `http://patft.uspto.gov/netacgi/nph-Parser?Sect1=PTO1&Sect2=HITOFF&d=PALL&p=1&u=%2Fnetahtml%2FPTO%2Fsrchnum.htm&r=1&f=G&l=50&s1=7171352.PN.&OS=PN/7171352&RS=PN/7171352`.

Su Chin Chang, Ravi C. Shahani, Domenic J. Cipollone, Michael V. Calcagno, Mari J. B. Olsen, and David J. Parkinson. 2010. Lexical Semantic Structure. 7,689,410. `http://patft.uspto.gov/netacgi/nph-Parser?Sect1=PTO1&Sect2=HITOFF&d=PALL&p=1&u=%2Fnetahtml%2FPTO%2Fsrchnum.htm&r=1&f=G&l=50&s1=7689410.PN.&OS=PN/7689410&RS=PN/7689410`.

Oana David and George Lakoff. 2013. Wikis, Beans and Cats: The Cascade Theory of Metaphor. In *12th International Cognitive Linguistics Conference (ICLC 12)*. Edmonton, Canada.

Oana David, George Lakoff, and Elise Stickles. 2016. Cascades in Metaphor and Grammar: A Case Study of Metaphors in the Gun Debate. *Constructions and Frames* 8(2):214–253.

Erik-Lân Do Dinh and Iryna Gurevych. 2016. Token-Level Metaphor Detection using NeuralNetworks. In *Proceedings of The Fourth Workshop on Metaphor in NLP, Association for Computational Linguistics / San Diego, CA, 17 June 2016*. pages 28–33.

Ellen Dodge, Jisup Hong, and Elise Stickles. 2015. MetaNet: Deep Semantic Automatic Metaphor Analysis. In *Proceedings of the Third Workshop on Metaphor in NLP*. Association for Computational Linguistics, pages 40–49.

Bonnie J. Dorr. 1993. *Machine Translation: A View from the Lexicon*. MIT Press, Cambridge, MA.

Bonnie J. Dorr. 1997. Large-Scale Dictionary Construction for Foreign Language Tutoring and Interlingual Machine Translation. *Machine Translation* 12:271–322.

Bonnie J. Dorr, Mari Olsen, Nizar Habash, and Scott Thomas. 2001. LCS Verb Database Documentation. `http://www.umiacs.umd.edu/~bonnie/Demos/LCS_Database_Documentation.html`.

Bonnie J. Dorr and Mari Broman Olsen. 1997. Deriving Verbal and Compositional Lexical Aspect for NLP Application. In *Proceedings of the 35th Annual Meeting of the Association for Computational Linguistics and Eighth Conference of the European Chapter of the Association for Computational Linguistics*, pages 151–158.

David Dowty. 1979. *Word Meaning and Montague Grammar*. Reidel, Dordrecht.

Dedre Gentner. 2001. Spatial Metaphor in Temporal Reasoning.

M. Guerssel, K. Hale, M. Laughren, B. Levin, and J. White Eagle. 1985. A Cross-linguistic Study of Transitivity Alternations. In W. H. Eilfort and P. D. Kroeber nad K. L. Peterson, editor, *Papers from the Parasession in Causatives and Agentivity at the Twenty-first Regional meeting of the Chicago Linguistic Society*, pages 48–63.

Nizar Habash and Bonnie J. Dorr. 2002. Handling Translation Divergences: Combining Statistical and Symbolic Techniques in Generation-Heavy Machine Translation. In *Proceedings of the Fifth Conference of the Association for Machine Translation in the Americas*. Tiburon, CA, pages 84–93.

Nizar Habash, Bonnie J. Dorr, and Christof Monz. 2006. Challenges in Building an Arabic GHMT system with SMT Components. In *Proceedings of the 7th Conference of the Association for Machine Translation in the Americas*. Boston, MA, pages 56–65.

Ray Jackendoff. 1983. *Semantics and Cognition*. MIT Press, Cambridge, MA.

Ray Jackendoff. 1990. *Semantic Structures*. MIT Press, Cambridge, MA.

Ray Jackendoff. 1996. The Proper Treatment of Measuring Out, Telicity, and Perhaps Even Quantification in English. *Natural Language and Linguistic Theory* 14:305–354.

Karin Kipper, Anna Korhonen, Neville Ryant, and Martha Palmer. 2007. A Large-scale Classification of English Verbs. In *Language Resources and Evaluation*.

George Lakoff and Mark Johnson. 1980. *Metaphors we live by*. Univ. of Chicago Press, Chicago.

Beth Levin. 1993. *English Verb Classes and Alternations: A Preliminary Investigation*. The University of Chicago Press.

Gina Levow, Bonnie J. Dorr, and Dekang Lin. 2000. Construction of Chinese-English Semantic Hierarchy for Cross-language Retrieval .

Yair Neuman, Dan Assaf, Yohai Cohen, Mark Last, Shlomo Argamon, Newton Howard, and Ophir Frieder. 2013. Metaphor Identification in Large Texts Corpora. `http://journals.plos.org/plosone/article?id=10.1371/journal.pone.0062343`.

Yair Neuman, Dan Assaf, Yohai Cohen, Mark Last, Shlomo Argamon, Newton Howard, and Ophir Frieder. 2018. MetaNet Metaphor Wiki, Version updated 3 January. `https://metaphor.icsi.berkeley.edu/pub/en/index.php/MetaNet_Metaphor_Wiki`.

Mari Broman Olsen. 1994. The Semantics and Pragmatics of Lexical and Grammatical Aspect. *Studies in the Linguistic Sciences* 24(1–2):361–375.

Mari Broman Olsen, Bonnie J. Dorr, and Scott Thomas. 1997. Toward Compact Monotonically Compositional Interlingua Using Lexical Aspect. In *Proceedings of the Workshop on Interlinguas in MT*. San Diego, CA, pages 33–44.

Martha Palmer, Claire Bonial, and Jena D. Hwang. 2017. VerbNet: Capturing English Verb behavior, Meaning and Usage.

Elise Stickles, Oana David, and Eve Sweetser. 2015. Grammatical Constructions, Frame Structure, and Metonymy: Their Contributions to Metaphor Computation. In *Proceedings of the 11th Meeting of the High Desert Linguistics Society (HDLS)*. pages 317–345.

Leonard Talmy. 1985. Lexicalization patterns; Semantic Structure in Lexical Forms 3:56–149.

David Traum and Nizar Habash. 2000. Generation from Lexical Conceptual Structures. In *Proceedings of the Workshop on Applied Interlinguas, North American Association for Computational Linguistics / Applied NLP Conference*. pages 34–41.

Yorick Wilks. 1995. Language, Vision and Metaphor. *Artificial Intelligence Review* 9:273–289.

A Supplemental Material: Metaphor Classes, Examples, LCSs

A supplemental resource (spreadsheet) has been provided in .zip format at:

```
https://www.dropbox.com/s/
4vm0ddulemcbnoa/NAACL-2018_Camera_
Ready_Metaphor_Classes.zip?dl=0
```

The top level file inside of the .zip file above is:

```
20180314-Final_Metaphor_Classes&Examples&
LCSs(NAACL-18).htm
```

This is a worksheet that contains two tabs, covering both Spatial Classes and Mappings into LCS structures for literal and metaphorical meanings:

- **Tab 1:** Spatial Classes - 16 spatial classes, divided according to 139 unique spatial expressions, with members corresponding to 197 hyperlinked MN metaphors. MN Metaphor categories that have been mapped into LCS structures in Tab 2 are listed at the top of each class in column B and highlighted in orange.

- **Tab 2:** LCS Mappings - Mappings from 16 spatial classes into LCS structures for both the physical/literal meaning and the metaphorical meaning. Includes examples, variables and constants, sample verbs, and

hyperlinks to the relevant MN metaphor cases. Examples in Column I are either found on the web (links provided) or adapted from the *Push* sentences.

Representing Spatial Relations in FrameNet

Miriam R. L. Petruck   **Michael Ellsworth**
International Computer Science Institute
Berkeley, California
`{miriamp, infinity}@icsi.berkeley.edu`

Abstract

While humans use natural language to express spatial relations between and across entities in the world with great facility, natural language systems have a facility that depends on that human facility. This position paper presents **FrameNet**'s[1] approach to representing spatial relations in language, and advocates its adoption for representing the meaning of spatial language. This work shows the importance of axis-orientation systems for capturing the complexity of spatial relations, which FrameNet encodes with semantic types.

1 Introduction

While humans use natural language to express spatial relations across entities in the world with great facility, natural language systems have a facility that depends on that human facility. (See (Mikolov et al., 2013) for a different perspective.) Natural Language Processing (NLP) applications such as robotic systems responding to commands about objects in a scene require accurate information on the spatial relations among those objects. In addition to determining *what* information to provide is the challenge of determining *how* to represent such information. This work presents the Frame Semantics view on representing spatial language, specifically as given in FrameNet (FN).

The rest of this position paper is organized as follows; Section 2 presents basic information about FN, including its current status; Section 3 provides a brief overview of related work; Section 4 covers the different kinds of spatial information that FN has recorded, including semantic types for characterizing spatial relation language, two of which constitute innovations over prior work; Section 5 shows how employing FN's spatial information can benefit NLP; and Section 6 briefly discusses FrameNet's plans for future work on the language of spatial relations. Importantly, expanding FN's coverage for representing spatial relations is possible given existing FN infrastructure, i.e. frames, frame elements, and frame-to-frame relations, as well as semantic types.

2 Background to FrameNet

This section provides a very brief overview of FN, with information about its foundational principles and its relatively recent attention to basic linguistic phenomena that pose challenges to NLP, including the language of spatial relations, as well as details about its current status.

2.1 Frame Semantics and FrameNet

Frame Semantics (Fillmore, 1985) is the theoretical basis of **FrameNet** (Ruppenhofer et al., 2016), a knowledge base building effort, whose product, the FN database, is useful in NLP applications.

Central to the theory is the **semantic frame** (Fillmore, 1975), a schematic representation of a scene, whose frame elements (**FEs**), or semantic roles, identify participants and other conceptual entities, and whose underlying conceptual structure humans access for both encoding and decoding purposes. FrameNet adopted the lexical unit (**LU**) as the focus of analysis, defining an LU as a pairing of a lemma and a frame (Cruse, 1986).

FrameNet also distinguishes core and non-core frame elements. Thus, **core FE**s uniquely define a frame: BUYER, SELLER, MONEY, and GOODS[2] uniquely define frames that constitute the `Commercial_transaction`[3] family of frames. In contrast, **non-core FE**s are relevant to events or situations in general; all events and situations occur at a time and in a place. The non-core

---

[1] http://framenet.icsi.berkeley.edu

[2] Frame Element names appear in SMALL CAPS.
[3] Frame names appear in `typewriter` font.

Proceedings of the First International Workshop on Spatial Language Understanding (SpLU-2018), pages 41–45
New Orleans, Louisiana, June 6, 2018. ©2018 Association for Computational Linguistics

FE PLACE is of particular importance for spatial relations (and is discussed further below).

FrameNet defines `Spatial_contact` as a scene in which a FIGURE is located in contact with a GROUND. With some words, the FIGURE is also asserted as fully or partially supported by the GROUND (e.g. *on*), while in others a support relation is denied (e.g., **TO**, as in *She put her hand TO the wall*), or unspecified (e.g. *against*). Some LUs assert a direction in which to find the FIGURE from the GROUND (e.g., *atop*).

Consider the two example sentences below that instantiate the `Spatial_contact` frame, where each realizes the FIGURE and the GROUND FEs.

1. Then [Maria ₗFIGURE] fell and lay **ON** [the floor GROUND].

2. There were [a hat and feathers FIGURE] **ATOP** [the lid GROUND].

Contrast *on* and *atop*: *on* allows any direction of contact (*on the {ceiling, wall, ground}*), while *atop* specifies a particular direction of contact, i.e., above the GROUND. FN encodes such differences in a set of semantic types that specify axis systems and directions, based on these axis systems.

2.2 Current Status of FrameNet

At the time of this writing, the FN database holds over 1,220 frames, 13,640 LUs, and nearly 202,230 annotated sentences. Of importance here, FrameNet has defined 29 spatial language frames, covering 409 LUs that describe spatial relations, and approximately 4,200 annotated sentences, along with six semantic types for distinguishing spatial relation LUs.

3 Related Work

Linguists, computational linguists, and NLP researchers in particular, have studied spatial relations in language, and for the sake of developing annotation schema and NLP systems that take such information into consideration.

For example, (Dorr and Voss, 1993), addressed spatial relations for defining the relation between an interlingua and a system for representing knowledge in machine translation. Pursuing machine translation (Voss et al., 1998) investigaged *how* the semantics of a spatial expression is allocated lexically.

(Jackendoff, 1996) considered how language users talk about what they see, addressing how the mind might encode spatial information and linguistic information, as well how it might communicate between the two. That work also laid out some of the "boundary conditions for a satisfactory answer to these questions" (1996:3), and defined an approach to spatial representation. In a somewhat similar vein (as a contributiton to cognitive semantic theory of conceptual structure), albeit from a different perspective, (Talmy, 2003) presented an approach to spatial representation that encompasses spoken and signed language.

More practically-oriented recent work (Kipper et al., 2004) expanded a verb lexicon (Kipper et al., 2000) using prepositions, i.e., linguistic material that encodes spatial information, extrapolating information about classes of verbs and their syntactic frames from (Levin, 1993). The annotation of spatial relations in language (Pustejovsky et al., 2011) constituted the focus of a workshop on interoperable semantic annotation, and included work on spatial role labeling with an eye toward extracting spatial information from corpora (Kordjamshidi et al., 2011) that also led to multimodal spatial role labeling (Kordjamshidi et al., 2017).

4 Spatial Information in FrameNet

This section describes the kind of information that FN provides about spatial relations, i.e., frames that characterize spatial relations, non-core FEs that indicate location of an event or an entity, frame-to-frame relations that link the relevant frames, and semantic types that give specific semantic information beyond a frame description or a LU definition.

4.1 Non-Core Frame Elements

An advantage of FrameNet as a resource for spatial language is that FN also models non-spatial language. This feature is especially important since spatial and non-spatial language are not completely separable. Most frames in FrameNet include one or more spatial FEs, the most common of which are PLACE, present in all frames that inherit from `Event`, as in # 3, and LOCATION_OF_PROTAGONIST, available in all frames with a causal entity (e.g. CAUSE) as in # 4, or a perceiver (e.g. EXPERIENCER).

3. The hiker **DIED** [in Antarctica PLACE].

4. She **TESTED** the bomb [from a safe distance LOCATION_OF_PROTAGONIST].

4.2 Frames and Frame Relations

Frames represent situations and states of affairs at a level of generalization that recognizes the commonalities within and across sets of semantically related lexical items. FN records several frame-to-frame relations to indicate how frames relate to each other in its hierarchy of frames; **Inheritance** and **Using** are the relevant ones for spatial relations language. Frames that *inherit* `Locative_relation` capture the lexical material for spatial relations in English.[4]

Inheritance exists between a parent frame and a child frame under specific circumstances: for each FE, frame relation, and semantic characteristic in the parent, the same or a more specific corresponding entity in the child exists, as in the relationship between `Locative_relation` and `Interior_profile_relation`. Using is a relationship between a child frame and parent frame in which only some of the FEs in the parent have a corresponding entity in the child; if such exist, they are more specific. Using holds between `Interior_profile_relation` and `Bounded_region`.

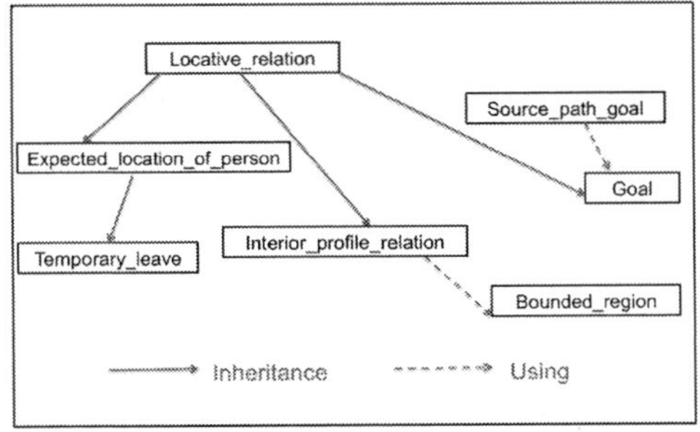

Figure 1: Inheritance and Using Relations

Figure 1 depicts some frames related to the `Locative_relation` frame via Inheritance, some of which also employ the Using relationship. Note that a frame may inherit one frame and use another: `Goal` inherits `Locative_relation` and uses `Source_path_goal`.[5]

The static spatial relations frames inherit from `Locative_relation`, which defines the basic situation where the FIGURE entity has a location that is determined by means of a relation to the GROUND, another entity. These static spatial relations all share this basic structure; moreover, each specific frame also holds a *Using* relation to an image schema[6] that defines the relation between the FIGURE and the GROUND.

FrameNet models the lexical unit *in* as a member of the `Interior_profile_relation` frame (which inherits `Locative_relation`). Its frame elements include FIGURE, the located entity and GROUND, the basis of the location. `Interior_profile_relation` uses the `Bounded_region` image schema, which defines a boundary, an inside, and an outside. Part of *Using* specifies that the FIGURE identifies the inside region, and the GROUND identifies the boundary. FN distinguishes among other LUs by defining them in different related frames in this family (of frames) and via semantic types that cross-cut frame distinctions.

4.3 Semantic Types

Linguists, anthropologists, and computer scientists have studied the cognitive, cultural, linguistic, and computational aspects of space and spatial relations for decades (Herskovitz, 1987; Bowerman and Pederson, 1992; Regier, 1996; Levinson, 2003). FrameNet has defined a cognitively-inspired set of semantic types for spatial LUs to indicate (1) with respect to which axis-system(s) (Talmy, 2000) a given LU is defined, and (2) which direction(s) from these axes the active zone a given LU selects.

	Semantic Type	**Example**
Basic Axis System	absolute	to the east of Pam
	viewpoint-based	to the left of Sue
	motion-based	ahead of Paul
	ground-based	to Chuck's left
FN Added	Near_absolute	atop the tree
	Flexible	in front of her

Table 1: Semantic Types for Spatial Relations

As Table 1 shows, the basic axis systems include four types: **absolute** (*to the east of X*); **viewpoint-based** (*to the left of X*); **motion-based** (*ahead of X*); and **ground-based** (*to X's left*). FrameNet has defined a semantic type for each of these four possibilities. Besides semantic types

---

[4] `https://tinyurl.com/y7jpt9hd`. FN team members are well-aware that the work has only begun.

[5] The careful reader will note the "incorrect" direction of the arrows in Figure 1, which follows conventions that FrameNet uses.

[6] Image schemas (Lakoff and Johnson, 1980) are cognitive models, such as of containment, oppositional forces, and verticality, which language users apply to understand and reason about the world. FN characterized image schemas as frames.

named with the terminology of the basic axis systems, FN has defined two other **new** semantic types: **Near_absolute** (*atop*) and **Flexible** (*in front*). These two semantic types innovate on previous work (Talmy, 2000), and derive from FN's fairly recent work on spatial relations.

Using semantic types for each direction in each axis system would seem like a simple enough modeling choice. However, LUs exhibit patterns whereby a default axis system is overridden under specific conditions. Thus, for example, some LUs inflexibly select an absolute direction (e.g., *east*); some normally select an absolute direction, but allow a ground-based one (*atop*); and some default to a ground-based direction, but allow viewpoint-based or motion-based direction (*in front*). FrameNet's semantic types specify the pattern of axis ambiguity a LU exhibits.

5 Operationalization

FrameNet's models of spatial language consist of frames, frame relations, and semantic types, all static and abstract. However, using FrameNet's models for visual scene understanding requires grounded and flexible implementations. As such, the machinery needed to match a spatial description like *the cow **IN FRONT** of the train* to an image requires the following: (1) object recognition of the GROUND (train); (2) image parsing for each axis system centered on the train (since *in front* is a flexible lexical unit); and (3) recognition of the FIGURE (cow) in the forward-pointing vector for each axis system.

Figure 2: the cow in front of the train

FrameNet contributes in three critical ways to this matching process, by providing the following:

1. training data showing the manifestation of the FIGURE and GROUND roles in language;

2. an inventory of frames for spatial situations that any system must recognize (e.g. `Containment`, `Contact`);

3. an inventory of semantic types for axis systems and their vectors.

Crucially, FrameNet's semantic types distinguish the flexible LU *in front* from a Motion_based LU (*ahead*), where only the motion-based forward zone of the train is scanned.

6 Future Work

This position paper has described FrameNet's work on static spatial relations. It has shown that FN provides critical information for certain NLP applications that require input for the processing of spatial relations language.

Going forward and with sufficient resources, FrameNet plans to analyze other types of spatial relations language, including the following:

- Dynamic spatial relations language, e.g. *to*, *from*, as in:

  She went **TO** the lake **FROM** the house.

  Pseudo-dynamic spatial relations, e.g. *across*, as in:

  She lives **ACROSS** the bridge.

- Constructions (Kay and Fillmore, 1999; Fillmore, 2013) that license static spatial relations to be construed as GOALs, as in:

  I went **UNDER** the bridge.

Preliminary studies of the other types of spatial language indicate that FN's existing system of frames, frame elements, frame-to-frame relations, and semantic types will serve as a solid foundation for future work.

References

Melissa Bowerman and Eric Pederson. 1992. Topological relations picture series. In Stephen C. Levinson, editor, *Space Stimuli Kit 1.2*. Max Planck Institute for Psycholinguistics, Nijmegen.

D.A. Cruse. 1986. *Lexical Semantics*. Cambridge University Press, Cambridge, UK.

Bonnie J. Dorr and Clare R. Voss. 1993. Machine translation of spatial expressions: Defining the relation between an interlingua and a knowledge representation system. In *Proceedings of the 11th National Conference on Artificial Intelligence. Washington, DC, USA, July 11-15, 1993.*, pages 374–379.

Charles J. Fillmore. 1975. An alternative to checklist theories of meaning. *Proceedings of the First Annual Meeting of the Berkeley Linguistics Society*, 1:123–131.

Charles J Fillmore. 1985. Frames and the semantics of understanding. *Quaderni di semantica*, 6(2):222–254.

Charles J. Fillmore. 2013. Berkeley construction grammar. In Thomas Hoffmann and Graeme Trousdale, editors, *Oxford Handbook of Construction Grammar*. Oxford University Press, Oxford.

Annette Herskovitz. 1987. *Language and Spatial Cognition: An interdisciplinary study of the prepositions in English*. Studies in Natural Language Processing. Cambridge University Press, Cambridge.

Ray Jackendoff. 1996. The architecture of the linguistic-spatial interface. In P. Bloom, M. Peterson, L. Nadel, and M. Garrett, editors, *Language and Space*, pages 1–30. MIT Press, Cambridge.

Paul Kay and Charles J. Fillmore. 1999. Grammatical constructions and linguistic generalizations: The what's x doing y? construction. *Language*, 75(1):1–33.

Karin Kipper, Hoa Trang Dang, and Martha Palmer. 2000. Class-based construction of a verb lexicon. In *Proceedings of the Seventeenth National Conference on Artificial Intelligence and Twelfth Conference on Innovative Applications of Artificial Intelligence*, pages 691–696. AAAI Press.

Karin Kipper, Benjamin Snyder, and Martha Palmer. 2004. Using prepositions to extend a verb lexicon. *Proceedings of the HLT/NAACL Workshop on Computational Lexical Semantics*, pages 23–29.

Kordjamshidi, Parisa, Martijn Van Otterlo, and Marie-Francine Moens. 2011. Spatial role labeling: Towards extraction of spatial relations from natural language. *ACM Trans. Speech Lang. Process.*, 8(3):4:1–4:36.

Parisa Kordjamshidi, Taher Rahgooy, Marie-Francine Moens, James Pustejovsky, Umar Manzoor, and Kirk Roberts. 2017. Clef 2017: Multimodal spatial role labeling (msprl) task overview. In Jones G. et al., editor, *Lecture Notes in Computer Science, vol. 10456*, pages 367–377. Springer, Cham.

George Lakoff and Mark Johnson. 1980. *Metaphors we Live by*. University of Chicago Press, Chicago.

Beth Levin. 1993. *English Verb Classes and Alternations: A Preliminary Investigation*. University of Chicago Press, Chicago.

Stephen C. Levinson. 2003. *Space in Language and Cognition: Explorations in Cognitive Diversity*. Language Culture and Cognition. Cambridge University Press.

Tomas Mikolov, Ilya Sutskever, Kai Chen, Greg S Corrado, and Jeff Dean. 2013. Distributed representations of words and phrases and their compositionality. In C. J. C. Burges, L. Bottou, M. Welling, Z. Ghahramani, and K. Q. Weinberger, editors, *Advances in Neural Information Processing Systems 26*, pages 3111–3119. Curran Associates, Inc.

James Pustejovsky, Jessica L Moszkowicz, and Marc Verhagen. 2011. Iso-space: The annotation of spatial information in language. *Proceedings of the Sixth Joint ISO-ACL SIGSEM Workshop on Interoperable Semantic Annotation*, 6:1–9.

Terry Regier. 1996. *The Human Semantic Potential: Spatial Language and Constrained Connectionism*. Language, Speech, and Communication. MIT Press, Cambridge, MA.

Josef Ruppenhofer, Michael Ellsworth, Miriam R. L. Petruck, Christopher R. Johnson, Collin F. Baker, and Jan Scheffczyk. 2016. *FrameNet II: Extended Theory and Practice*. ICSI: Berkeley.

Leonard Talmy. 2000. *Toward a Cognitive Semantics*. Language, Speech, and Communication. MIT Press, Cambridge, MA.

Leonard Talmy. 2003. The representation of spatial structure in spoken and signed language: A neural model. *Language and Linguistics*, 4(2):207–250.

Clare R. Voss, Bonnie J. Dorr, and M. Ulku Sencan. 1998. Lexical allocation in interlingua-based machine translation of spatial expressions. In Patrick Olivier and Klaus-Peter Gapp, editors, *Representation and Processing of Spatial Expressions*, pages 133–148. Psychology Press.

Points, Paths, and Playscapes: Large-scale Spatial Language Understanding Tasks Set in the Real World

Jason Baldridge   Tania Bedrax-Weiss   Daphne Luong   Srini Naryanan
Bo Pang   Fernando Pereira   Radu Soricut   Michael Tseng   Yuan Zhang
Google Inc.
Mountain View, CA
{jridge,tbedrax,daphnel,srinin,bopang,pereira,
rsoricut,michaeltseng,zhangyua}@google.com

Abstract

Spatial language understanding is important for practical applications and as a building block for better abstract language understanding. Much progress has been made through work on understanding spatial relations and values in images and texts as well as on giving and following navigation instructions in restricted domains. We argue that the next big advances in spatial language understanding can be best supported by creating large-scale datasets that focus on points and paths based in the real world, and then extending these to create online, persistent playscapes that mix human and bot players, where the bot players must learn, evolve, and survive according to their depth of understanding of scenes, navigation, and interactions.

1 Introduction

Language is not sealed in a textual medium disconnected from the world. People use language to talk about people, places and things that exist both in time and space. Abstract ideas are typically conveyed through metaphors that are grounded in embodied concepts from the domains of spatial movement, forces, and manipulation (Naraynan, 1999). Mental simulation involving motor and perceptual content likely plays a crucial role in sentence comprehension (Bergen et al., 2010). Natural language understanding thus requires the ability to analyze complex descriptions that relate referents spatially and temporally and connect them to grounded locations and times.

One of the richest domains for encountering such language is that of providing and following navigational instructions involving both named and vague references and relationships in both indoor and outdoor contexts. Spatial navigation itself is one of the better understood aspects of cognitive function, including extensive research into cells that encode grids, boundaries and directions (Chersi and Burgess, 2015; Moser et al., 2017). This indicates that work on spatial tasks in language has the potential to lead to a virtuous cycle between modeling of language and understanding of the brain and cognition.

No current systems adequately support natural language interactions for spatial tasks. Geospatial mapping applications (such as Google Maps) provide algorithmic, route-based instruction at a global scale. However, they rely on explicitly named roads, paths, and addresses, and they assume a large database as a model of the world, which includes mappings between names and geo locations. Such systems give instructions but cannot interpret them, much less interact with a human user. They also typically do poorly at providing contextual descriptions, especially for buildings, bridges, and other salient landmarks.

Understanding spatial references from natural language must handle inherent spatial vagueness and other features of the figure, and ground objects or trajectories in a coordinate system. Spatial grounding is relative—it depends on size, shape, and function of the figure and ground objects. Furthermore, it is identified by transforming location with respect to reference frames in language (Levinson, 2003; Tenbrink and Kuhn, 2011) to a ground. Languages have many options for describing the spatial relationships between different participants and objects and these must be reconciled with the ground- truth scene or map.

We argue that the next big advances in spatial language understanding can be best enabled by first creating large-scale datasets (hundreds of thousand to millions of examples) that require spatial understanding of real world points and paths, and next, building on these to create persistent, online playscapes that enable both automated agents and people to interact in virtual and augmented re-

Proceedings of the First International Workshop on Spatial Language Understanding (SpLU-2018), pages 46–52
New Orleans, Louisiana, June 6, 2018. ©2018 Association for Computational Linguistics

ality environments.

Navigation involves traversal through a series of points, and each point can involve detailed scene understanding needs. Navigation is also an excellent link between the local (e.g., within a building) and the global (e.g., across a continent) variants of spatial tasks. Scene understanding—in both images and texts—is needed at both ends of this scale and in between. We expect that such a project provides challenges of high complexity, while also linking in to rich, already-available resources that connect both text and images to each other and to key metadata, including coordinates in both space and time.

2 Pillars and Principles

Here are some considerations as we begin a multi-year effort to create these resources.

2.1 Data and annotation

Our goal is to create large-scale resources that encompass natural spatially oriented tasks that ordinary people accomplish every day.

Scale To be able to work with diverse locations (e.g., cities, theme parks, natural settings) across the world, we need large datasets associating language with spatially relevant points and paths—on the scale of *at least hundreds of thousands*.

Multilinguality For both theoretical and practical reasons, we cannot focus on just one language. Different languages have different spatial relations, often involving the three different frames of reference—relative, intrinsic, and absolute (Levinson, 2003)—in different ways. Navigational systems supporting vague reference off the grid are needed even more in locations where English and other majority languages are not spoken.

One way we already target multilinguality is via community-driven crowd-sourcing (Funk et al., 2018). In our approach, we intentionally cycle our iterations throughout the world and we involve developers from each locale because they have insights into how the local context affects how language is used and how the task is performed.

User-driven annotation We seek to complement previous efforts that have focused on fine-grained linguistic annotation, such as Iso-Space (Pustejovsky, 2017). We will obtain scale through both crowd-sourcing and gaming environments—that is, annotations that can be derived from com-petent language speakers (Chang et al., 2016). This places an emphasis on task evaluations with implicit feedback rather than prediction and evaluation of labels on text and images. Spatial tasks are natural fits for this strategy, since both evaluation metrics and reward functions (in reinforcement learning) can use spatial proximity to an end location (MacMahon et al., 2006; Chen and Mooney, 2011; Vogel and Jurafsky, 2010; Artzi and Zettlemoyer, 2013) or spatial configuration (Bisk et al., 2018; Misra et al., 2017; Tan and Bansal, 2018).

There are trade-offs between *model-driven* and *user-driven* corpus building. The former defines inventories of spatial relations and generating assignments that will cover them. This may omit phenomena or distinctions not covered in the model and requires considerable expertise and tooling—both of which increase cost and limit scale. User-driven annotation is more exploratory and may be limited by the preferences and tendencies of contributors. We will mitigate such effects by composing diverse crowds from various locales (Funk et al., 2018). Ultimately, we seek to create resources that contain language grounded in spatial relations that, by construction, include extra-linguistic factors like vantage point, shared context, and other location-dependent world knowledge. We also expect this setting to support complementary non-linguistic spatial understanding approaches, such as Simultaneous Localization and Mapping (Cadena et al., 2016).

Sharing and privacy To facilitate accessibility and reproducibility, the source material used for building resources should be, wherever possible, unencumbered by copyright and be acquired with full permission from content creators. Location information brings with it significant privacy and ethical considerations. We will thus focus on locations in shared public spaces that avoid close connections to any person who helps create the data. We will develop our datasets using open resources such as Wikipedia and Open Street Maps combined with materials produced by (both paid and volunteer) crowd contributors who have granted permission in advance. Overall, our datasets and environments will be built—from start to finish—to be compliant with the European Union's General Data Protection Regulation (Council of European Union, 2016).[1]

---

[1] https://www.eugdpr.org/

2.2 Task considerations

We emphasize the real world as the basis for spatial language understanding tasks, while allowing for a spectrum of resources from digitized real world artifacts to virtual environments to augmented real world interactions.

Real world emphasis. The natural starting point for building spatial language understanding capabilities is the real world itself. For example, spoken interfaces to mobile robots necessarily integrate vague reference and learning a local map through exploration (Thomason et al., 2015; Hanheide et al., 2017; Arkin et al., 2017). Unfortunately, working with physical robots brings additional challenges such as dealing with hardware calibration and failure. Thus, many researchers have opted instead to work with simulated environments that enable faster iteration on modeling and learning (Jänner et al., 2017; Hermann et al., 2017; Bisk et al., 2018), and some support both movement and manipulation (Yan et al., 2018).

Simulated environments, however, do not represent full real world messiness. It is thus interesting to consider a middle ground: working with high-fidelity simulations of the real world. For example, Anderson et al. (2017) introduce a visually grounded navigation task set in 3D simulations of actual houses. This requires both rich scene understanding and difficult language interpretation. We intend to work in this same mode, gathering digitized artifacts relating to real world locations—including databases, texts, images, and more—to support complex and compelling tasks that can impact real world applications. In particular, we expect to achieve considerable scale on navigational tasks for walking through a campus or park.

First-person perspective. For at least some of the tasks we envision, human and machine agents will not have access to a God's eye view, like that available to mapping applications (with access to full geographic features via databases). Instead, such tasks must be solvable by interpreting visual and textual stimuli relevant to the locations. This should put a greater emphasis on challenging spatial descriptions and relationships rather than known and named routes. Nonetheless, maps as visual artifacts (e.g., PDFs) may be incorporated in some cases, giving automated agents the ability to use them as a hiker might use a paper map without access to a GPS-based mapping application.

Mirowski et al. (2018) is a recent example that takes a first-person perspective in a real world simulation, though one that does not incorporate language. They learn a model for navigating the Google Street View graph via reinforcement learning, where the goal location is specified via its distance to several other landmark locations and no explicit maps are used. Two especially interesting aspects of their approach are their use of curriculum learning (start with nearby goals and then tackle more distant ones) and showing successful adaptation from one city to another. These ideas are complementary to those that use language as a component in learning to navigate, so it should be possible to effectively integrate linguistic inputs (e.g., directions and descriptions of the goal) into the approach.

Human–machine interaction Thomason et al. (2015) demonstrate a robot that interacts with people and incrementally expands its language understanding capabilities. In this vein, we seek to create simulated (real world) environments that support spatial language tasks in which bots and humans mix, collaborate, and compete. In such settings, there is no annotation: instead, players–both bot and human–gain points, status, and bounty (e.g., compute credits) by accomplishing goals.

This approach opens up opportunities to transition from static tasks such as following a particular set of navigational instructions to dynamic interactions such as following instructions made in the moment and in context by another player. If successful, this dynamism could create far greater scale for iterating on modeling ideas—with the evaluation measure (success in the game) as a built-in feature. This approach not only frees us from the need for costly, one-off annotation efforts, but also creates an ecologically compelling environment where progress is forced on and by the bots: they must perform well to get rewards to stay alive and maintain their status in the playscape (such as compute credits). As importantly, this survival criterion also entails the need to attend to representational and computational efficiency (FLOPS) on top of overall ability.

Building playscapes also plots a path from virtual real world to augmented reality applications and games that include linguistic interactions between human and bot players, and manipulation of virtual objects that have real world locations. Capturing Pokémon characters and interacting with gyms in Pokémon Go are examples of such manipulations.

3 Tasks

Our focus on real world spatial language artifacts provides a natural and mutually reinforcing progression from points to paths to playscapes.

Points Scene understanding—building a model for a point in space—is the bedrock of real world spatial language tasks. We must be able to observe and describe visible objects and the spatial relationships between them. Before addressing paths and navigation tasks, we can make considerable progress by improving our data and modeling for spatial relations in tasks like image segmentation and image captioning (Hall et al., 2011; Hürlimann and Bos, 2016), grounding referential expressions (Kazemzadeh et al., 2014; Mao et al., 2016; Hu et al., 2017), relative positioning of objects (Kitaev and Klein, 2017) and image geolocation (Hays and Efros, 2008; Zamir et al., 2016). We will create collaborative image identification and description tasks that emphasize spatial relations and geographically salient landmarks.

There has also been much work on annotating and calculating spatial relations in text (Pustejovsky et al., 2015; Pustejovsky, 2017), resolving toponyms (Leidner, 2007; DeLozier et al., 2015), and text geolocation (Wing and Baldridge, 2014; Rahimi et al., 2017). There are further opportunities for building or exploiting annotations on spatially focused texts—e.g., identifying vague regions (DeLozier et al., 2016) or writing a WikiVoyage page for a city given all available information in Wikipedia, akin to Liu et al. (2018).

Most importantly, the extensive mappings we have between texts and images and their corresponding locations motivate a focus on simulations of the real world. Learning spatial relations within massive amounts of images and texts can serve as a pretraining step to building components of models that solve real world navigation tasks.

Paths Understanding salient features and spatial relations in images and text naturally extends into navigation tasks that connect such points. To avoid biases, we will create navigation challenges through several different means, with an emphasis on domains that require a mix of named features, salient landmarks, and general features that necessitate relational, imprecise reference.

Harvesting and extending: There are numerous, extensive walking tours of public spaces. For example, universities typically provide self-guided campus tours that include text, images, and maps. Considerable work is required to standardize the specification and formatting of the tours, organize the associated artifacts (such as pictures), and convert the analog paths to digital ones (or create them) so that they could be used in experiments.

Descriptions to paths: In other cases, we have human descriptions of journeys in resources like WikiVoyage, such as from airports to city centers or how to get into Grand Canyon by car from different directions. We can have multiple people follow the directions in a resource like Google Street View to establish both ground truth and capture variation in human performance.

Paths to descriptions: Many volunteers on OpenStreetMaps produce GPS traces,[2] and we can elicit navigational instructions covering them.

Points to paths and descriptions: Given points, we can generate random paths, elicit navigational instructions for them, and then have others generate paths following instructions. This setup does not depend on existing data and gives more control over variables such as the number of points, length of the descriptions, and more. It can also tie into existing point-based data, such as the Google Landmarks,[3] so that point and path models that reinforce each other can be explored.

This is the strategy we are beginning with: focusing on collecting navigational instructions in city centers, resorts and college campuses for itineraries that include three to ten points of interest. Itineraries will be generated both by sampling paths connecting waypoints drawn from gazeteers and Wikipedia and by generating travel itineraries from real world trips (Friggstad et al., 2018). We will collect instructions given both by people who are physically on the ground as well as others visiting the points virtually via Google Street View. We expect that this effort will go through several iterations as we discover the pain points and better understand which approaches work best.

Playscapes Collecting datasets with paths and corresponding navigation instructions can provide a valuable source for learning and evalu-

---

ating models. The HCRC MapTask (Anderson et al., 1991) is a launching-off point for creating collaborative games where participants help each other complete a virtual road rally. This naturally extends the path-oriented efforts discussed above, but mixes in collaboration and competition while providing motivation through in-game rewards (e.g., status, points, and compute credits). Such games could take a variety of forms: one possibility is to provide a series of waypoints drawn from a WikiVoyage page to one player who then uses the page and resources like Google Street View to write instructions. Another player (or players) must then follow the instructions and possibly solve additional puzzles or tasks along the way.

It would be even more powerful to create online, persistent games in which human and bot players need to understand multi-step natural language cues in order to find target locations and accomplish other in-game objectives. This moves us from creating datasets to establishing ecologically interesting playscapes, such as ones in which bots must solve navigation tasks in order to gain the rewards needed for their survival.

Here we focus on spatial motion and relations necessary for navigation and scene understanding. By embedding our tasks and playscapes in digitized versions of the real world, however, we provide a natural launching-off point for eventually adding manipulation via augmented reality applications. The recently released Google Maps gaming API[4] can be a significant enabling technology for creating such playscapes. A tantalizing prospect would be to create games akin to Ingress and Pokémon Go that furthermore involve language. The key would be to design them to be relevant, compelling and fun while ensuring privacy and safety.

Gamification also makes the playscape more compelling and fun for human participants. It gives a reason for participants to engage more with with other players and negotiate the spatial environment to achieve their in-game goals. We will likely assign asymmetric capabilities for both human and machine players. That is, players will take on different roles with different abilities— e.g., some could be scouts who have a wider range of (augmented) perception, while others could be

manipulators who can acquire objects and solve puzzles requiring interaction with virtual objects at game-relevant real world locations. Machine agents could play many different roles, such as fast virtual scouts, helpful carriers of virtual objects, and translators who help interactions between human players who speak different languages. Such an environment should also provide a rich substrate for exploring approaches that incorporate pragmatic inference for giving and following instructions (Fried et al., 2018).

In designing such playscapes, we will avoid violent themes and combatitive gameplay. Instead, we seek to design them in the mold of colloborative board games like Forbidden Island. Players may still compete for overall higher individual rankings with respect to status and points, but we envision that they will do this by individually contributing to collaborative group efforts.

4 Conclusion

We seek to create large-scale datasets that thread together tasks that present challenges from points to paths and ultimately provide the basis upon which we create playscapes that incorporate real world data and interactions. The annotations for these will be in the form of language and behaviors rather than detailed formal linguistic representations. However, we believe it is likely that successful models will avail themselves of structured information around ideas like reference frames, structural biases in planning and navigation, and more. We also would welcome additional layers of analysis on the data we release.

In sum, we seek to produce richly associated data that ties text and images to locations at local, global, and scene-level resolutions. We hope to get feedback from the community and build collaborations as we begin this endeavor.

Acknowledgments

We thank Igor Karpov, Slav Petrov, Michael Ringgaard, Chris Waterson, David Weiss and the anonymous reviewers for their valuable feedback.

References

A Anderson, M Bader, E Bard, E Boyle, G. M Doherty, S Garrod, S Isard, J Kowtko, J McAllister, J Miller, C Sotillo, H. S. Thompson, and R. Weinert. 1991. The HCRC Map Task Corpus. *Language and Speech*, 34:351–366.

---

[4]https://developers.google.com/maps/gaming/

Peter Anderson, Qi Wu, Damien Teney, Jake Bruce, Mark Johnson, Niko Sünderhauf, Ian D. Reid, Stephen Gould, and Anton van den Hengel. 2017. Vision-and-language navigation: Interpreting visually-grounded navigation instructions in real environments. *CoRR*, abs/1711.07280.

Jacob Arkin, Matthew R. Walter, Adrian Boteanu, Michael E. Napoli, Harel Biggie, Hadas Kress-Gazit, and Thomas M. Howard. 2017. Contextual awareness: Understanding monologic natural language instructions for autonomous robots. In *Proceedings of the IEEE International Symposium on Robot and Human Interactive Communication (RO-MAN)*.

Yoav Artzi and Luke Zettlemoyer. 2013. Weakly supervised learning of semantic parsers for mapping instructions to actions. *Transactions of the Association for Computational Linguistics*, 1(1):49–62.

Benjamin K. Bergen, Shane Lindsay, Teenie Matlock, and Srini Narayanan. 2010. Spatial and linguistic aspects of visual imagery in sentence comprehension. *Cognitive Science*, 31(5):733–764.

Yonatan Bisk, Kevin Shih, Yejin Choi, and Daniel Marcu. 2018. Learning interpretable spatial operations in a rich 3d blocks world. In *Proceedings of the Thirty-Second Conference on Artificial Intelligence (AAAI-18)*, New Orleans, USA.

C. Cadena, L. Carlone, H. Carrillo, Y. Latif, D. Scaramuzza, J. Neira, I. Reid, and J. J. Leonard. 2016. Past, present, and future of simultaneous localization and mapping: Toward the robust-perception age. *IEEE Transactions on Robotics*, 32(6):1309–1332.

Nancy Chang, Russell Lee-Goldman, and Michael Tseng. 2016. Linguistic wisdom from the crowd. In *Crowdsourcing Breakthroughs for Language Technology Applications*.

David L. Chen and Raymond J. Mooney. 2011. Learning to interpret natural language navigation instructions from observations. In *Proceedings of the 25th AAAI Conference on Artificial Intelligence (AAAI-2011)*, San Francisco, CA, USA.

Fabian Chersi and Neil Burgess. 2015. The cognitive architecture of spatial navigation: Hippocampal and striatal contributions. *Neuron*, 88(1):64 – 77.

Council of European Union. 2016. Regulation (EU) 2016/679 of the European Parliament and of the Council of 27 April 2016 on the protection of natural persons with regard to the processing of personal data and on the free movement of such data, and repealing Directive 95/46/EC (General Data Protection Regulation). *Official Journal of the European Union*, L119:1–88.

Grant DeLozier, Jason Baldridge, and Loretta London. 2015. Gazetteer-independent toponym resolution using geographic word profiles.

Grant DeLozier, Ben Wing, Jason Baldridge, and Scott Nesbit. 2016. Creating a novel geolocation corpus from historical texts. In *Proceedings of the 10th Linguistic Annotation Workshop held in conjunction with ACL 2016 (LAW-X 2016)*, pages 188–198, Berlin, Germany. Association for Computational Linguistics.

Daniel Fried, Jacob Andreas, and Dan Klein. 2018. Unified pragmatic models for generating and following instructions. In *Proceedings of NAACL-HLT 2018*.

Zachary Friggstad, Sreenivas Gollapudi, Kostas Kollias, Tamas Sarlos, Chaitanya Swamy, and Andrew Tomkins. 2018. Orienteering algorithms for generating travel itineraries. In *International Conference on Web Search and Data Mining (WSDM)*.

Christina Funk, Michael Tseng, Ravindran Rajakumar, and Linne Ha. 2018. Community-driven crowdsourcing: Data collection with local developers. In *Proceedings of the 11th Language Resources and Evaluation Conference (LREC)*, Miyazaki, Japan.

Mark Hall, Philip D Smart, and Christopher Jones. 2011. Interpreting spatial language in image captions. *Cognitive processing*, 12:67–94.

Marc Hanheide, Moritz Göbelbecker, Graham S. Horn, Andrzej Pronobis, Kristoffer Sj, Alper Aydemir, Patric Jensfelt, Charles Gretton, Richard Dearden, Miroslav Janicek, Hendrik Zender, Geert-Jan Kruijff, Nick Hawes, and Jeremy L. Wyatt. 2017. Robot task planning and explanation in open and uncertain worlds. *Artificial Intelligence*, 247:119 – 150. Special Issue on AI and Robotics.

James Hays and Alexei A. Efros. 2008. IM2GPS: estimating geographic information from a single image. In *2008 IEEE Computer Society Conference on Computer Vision and Pattern Recognition (CVPR 2008), 24-26 June 2008, Anchorage, Alaska, USA*.

Karl Moritz Hermann, Felix Hill, Simon Green, Fumin Wang, Ryan Faulkner, Hubert Soyer, David Szepesvari, Wojciech Marian Czarnecki, Max Jaderberg, Denis Teplyashin, Marcus Wainwright, Chris Apps, Demis Hassabis, and Phil Blunsom. 2017. Grounded language learning in a simulated 3d world. *CoRR*, abs/1706.06551.

Ronghang Hu, Marcus Rohrbach, Jacob Andreas, Trevor Darrell, and Kate Saenko. 2017. Modeling relationships in referential expressions with compositional modular networks. In *2017 IEEE Conference on Computer Vision and Pattern Recognition (CVPR)*, pages 4418–4427. IEEE.

Manuela Hürlimann and Johan Bos. 2016. Combining lexical and spatial knowledge to predict spatial relations between objects in images. In *Proceedings of the 5th Workshop on Vision and Language*, pages 10–18, Berlin, Germany. Association for Computational Linguistics.

Michaela Jänner, Karthik Narasimhan, and Regina Barzilay. 2017. Representation learning for grounded spatial reasoning. *CoRR*, abs/1707.03938.

Sahar Kazemzadeh, Vicente Ordonez, Mark Matten, and Tamara Berg. 2014. Referitgame: Referring to objects in photographs of natural scenes. In *Proceedings of the 2014 conference on empirical methods in natural language processing (EMNLP)*, pages 787–798.

Nikita Kitaev and Dan Klein. 2017. Where is misty? interpreting spatial descriptors by modeling regions in space. In *Proceedings of the 2017 Conference on Empirical Methods in Natural Language Processing*, pages 157–166, Copenhagen, Denmark. Association for Computational Linguistics.

Jochen L. Leidner. 2007. *Toponym Resolution in Text: Annotation, Evaluation and Applications of Spatial Grounding of Place Names*. Dissertations.com.

Stephen C. Levinson. 2003. *Space in Language and Cognition: Explorations in Cognitive Diversity*. Cambridge University Press.

Peter J. Liu, Mohammad Ahmad Saleh, Etienne Pot, Ben Goodrich, Ryan Sepassi, Lukasz Kaiser, and Noam Shazeer. 2018. Generating wikipedia by summarizing long sequences.

Matt MacMahon, Brian Stankiewicz, and Benjamin Kuipers. 2006. Walk the talk: Connecting language, knowledge, and action in route instructions. In *Proceedings of the 21st National Conference on Artificial Intelligence (AAAI-2006)*, pages 1475–1482, Boston, MA, USA.

Junhua Mao, Jonathan Huang, Alexander Toshev, Oana Camburu, Alan L Yuille, and Kevin Murphy. 2016. Generation and comprehension of unambiguous object descriptions. In *Proceedings of the IEEE conference on computer vision and pattern recognition*, pages 11–20.

Piotr Mirowski, Matthew Koichi Grimes, Mateusz Malinowski, Karl Moritz Hermann, Keith Anderson, Denis Teplyashin, Karen Simonyan, Koray Kavukcuoglu, Andrew Zisserman, and Raia Hadsell. 2018. Learning to navigate in cities without a map. *CoRR*, abs/1804.00168.

Dipendra Misra, John Langford, and Yoav Artzi. 2017. Mapping instructions and visual observations to actions with reinforcement learning. In *Proceedings of the 2017 Conference on Empirical Methods in Natural Language Processing*, pages 1015–1026. Association for Computational Linguistics.

Edvard Moser, May-Britt Moser, and Bruce Mcnaughton. 2017. Spatial representation in the hippocampal formation: A history. 20:1448–1464.

Srini Narayanan. 1999. Moving right along: A computational model of metaphoric reasoning about events. In *Proceedings of the National Conference on Artificial Intelligence*, pages 121–128, Orlando, Florida. AAAI Press.

James Pustejovsky. 2017. Iso-space: Annotating static and dynamic spatial information. In Nancy Ide and James Pustejovsky, editors, *Handbook of Linguistic Annotation*, pages 989–1024. Springer.

James Pustejovsky, Parisa Kordjamshidi, Marie-Francine Moens, Aaron Levine, Seth Dworman, and Zachary Yocum. 2015. Semeval-2015 task 8: Spaceeval. In *Proceedings of the 9th International Workshop on Semantic Evaluation (SemEval 2015)*, pages 884–894, Denver, Colorado. Association for Computational Linguistics.

Afshin Rahimi, Trevor Cohn, and Timothy Baldwin. 2017. A neural model for user geolocation and lexical dialectology. In *Proceedings of the 55th Annual Meeting of the Association for Computational Linguistics (Volume 2: Short Papers)*, pages 209–216, Vancouver, Canada. Association for Computational Linguistics.

Hao Tan and Mohit Bansal. 2018. Source-target inference models for spatial instruction understanding. In *Proceedings of the 32nd AAAI Conference on Artificial Intelligence*, New Orleans, Louisiana.

Thora Tenbrink and Werner Kuhn. 2011. A model of spatial reference frames in language. In *Spatial Information Theory*, pages 371–390, Berlin, Heidelberg. Springer Berlin Heidelberg.

Jesse Thomason, Shiqi Zhang, Raymond J Mooney, and Peter Stone. 2015. Learning to interpret natural language commands through human-robot dialog. In *IJCAI*, pages 1923–1929.

Adam Vogel and Daniel Jurafsky. 2010. Learning to follow navigational directions. In *Proceedings of the 48th Annual Meeting of the Association for Computational Linguistics*, pages 806–814, Uppsala, Sweden. Association for Computational Linguistics.

Benjamin Wing and Jason Baldridge. 2014. Hierarchical discriminative classification for text-based geolocation. In *Proceedings of the 2014 Conference on Empirical Methods in Natural Language Processing (EMNLP)*, pages 336–348, Doha, Qatar. Association for Computational Linguistics.

Claudia Yan, Dipendra Misra, Andrew Bennnett, Aaron Walsman, Yonatan Bisk, and Yoav Artzi. 2018. Chalet: Cornell house agent learning environment. *CoRR*, abs/1801.07357.

Amir R. Zamir, Asaad Hakeem, Luc Van Gool, Mubarak Shah, and Richard Szeliski. 2016. Introduction to large-scale visual geo-localization. In Amir R. Zamir, Asaad Hakeem, Luc Van Gool, Mubarak Shah, and Richard Szeliski, editors, *Large-Scale Visual Geo-Localization*, pages 1–18. Springer International Publishing.

Anaphora Resolution for Improving Spatial Relation Extraction from Text

Umar Manzoor* Parisa Kordjamshidi*†
*Tulane University, Computer Science Department, New Orleans, LA, USA
†Florida Institute for Human and Machine Cognition (IHMC), Pensacola, FL, USA
{umanzoor,pkordjam}@tulane.edu

Abstract

Spatial relation extraction from generic text is a challenging problem due to the ambiguity of the prepositions spatial meaning as well as the nesting structure of the spatial descriptions. In this work, we highlight the difficulties that the anaphora can make in the extraction of spatial relations. We use external multi-modal (here visual) resources to find the most probable candidates for resolving the anaphoras that refer to the landmarks of the spatial relations. We then use global inference to decide jointly on resolving the anaphora and extraction of the spatial relations. Our preliminary results show that resolving anaphora improves the state-of-the-art results on spatial relation extraction.

1 Introduction

Spatial relation extraction is the task of determining the relations that can exist among the spatial roles extracted from the text (D'Souza and Ng, 2015). In the recent years, significant progress has been made in spatial language understanding (i.e. mapping natural language text to a formal spatial meaning representation) (Kordjamshidi et al., 2017a; Kordjamshidi and Moens, 2015a). As a basic example consider the sentence, "A car is parked in front of a house." In this sentence *car* is a *trajector*, *house* is a *landmark* and *in front of* is a *spatial indicator*. Spatial indicators indicate the existence of spatial information in a sentence. Trajector is an entity whose location is described and landmark is a reference object for describing the location of a trajector.

Extraction of the spatial relations with a good accuracy is still challenging (Pustejovsky et al., 2015). Particularly, our investigation on the errors of the previous models shows that when in a sentence the landmark is expressed as a pronoun like *("it", "them", "him",..)*, the extraction of spatial relations becomes more difficult.

For example, in the sentence, *"A narrow, rising street with colourful houses on both sides, among them a green house with balconies and a white car parked in front of it, and a blue-and-white church on the right"*, some of the spatial relations for this sentence will contain a landmark which is a pronoun such as $\langle R_1 \leftarrow$[a green house]$_{tr}$, [among]$_{sp}$, [them]$_{lm}\rangle$ and $\langle R_2 \leftarrow$[a white car]$_{tr}$, [in front of]$_{sp}$, [it]$_{lm}\rangle$. This issue is related to the well-known *anaphora resolution* problem which is also problematic for our goal of spatial relation extraction.

Anaphora Resolution which mostly appears as pronoun resolution, is the linguistic phenomenon by which the given pronoun is interpreted with the help of earlier or later items in the discourse (Mitkov, 2005). The pronoun word/phrase is referred as anaphor whereas the word/phrase to which it is referring is called antecedent, as both anaphor and antecedent are referring to the same object in the real world, they are termed co-referential (Mitkov et al., 2007). It might be possible that for some anaphor, the antecedent is not mentioned in the same sentence, for example, consider a sentence, *"there are a couple of trees in front of it"*, here *"it"* is referring to some object which is not mentioned in the sentence, however, the referring object might have been mentioned in another sentence of the document. Anaphora Resolution generally is recognized as a difficult problem in Natural Language Processing (Lee et al., 2017a; Marasovic et al., 2017).

The main research questions that we aim to address in this paper are, 1) whether the external knowledge from multimodal resources can help anaphora resolution in text. 2) whether the anaphora resolution can help in the spatial relation extraction from text (especially the relations in the form of triplet - Trajector, Spatial Indicator, Landmark). To answer these questions, we incorpo-

53

Proceedings of the First International Workshop on Spatial Language Understanding (SpLU-2018), pages 53–62
New Orleans, Louisiana, June 6, 2018. ©2018 Association for Computational Linguistics

Figure 1: Image Textual Description: "A narrow, rising street with colourful houses on both sides, among them a green house with balconies and a white car parked in front of it, and a blue-and-white church on the right"

rated anaphora resolution for the pronouns in the sentence and proposed a global machine learning model to exploit the resolved pronouns. In the first step, we find the list of possible landmarks that can replace a pronoun in a relation (under consideration) with a specific candidate trajector and candidate spatial indicator. We used Visual Genome (Krishna et al., 2017) (an external) dataset for this purpose.

Visual genome dataset provides us a list of possible landmarks which can be used to resolve the anaphora by filtering them based on their similarity with the candidate landmarks that appear in the sentence. This information is used in the global inference model for joint prediction. We improve the spatial relation extraction from text by incorporating anaphora resolution to recognize landmarks in spatial relations which distinguishes our work from other works on anaphora resolution. The contribution of this paper includes a) exploiting external visual relation datasets to inject external knowledge into our models b) forming a joint model that imposes the consistency between the decisions made by separate relation classifiers that decide on a candidate spatial relation with pronoun landmark and candidate spatial relations with that pronoun replaced by candidate noun resolvants. c) obtaining state-of-the-art results on spatial information extraction by exploiting the anaphora resolution. This paper shows our preliminary efforts in the sense that we have not applied the existing work on anaphora resolution. We do not aim at improving the current techniques in that area but only show that such resolutions using visual resources can help spatial relation extraction.

The rest of this paper is organized as follows,

first we describe the problem setting in Section 2; our proposed model for this problem is described in Section 3. The dataset used in tests, and evaluation results, are presented in Section 4. In Section 5, we briefly point to the related work in this area. Finally, Section 6 summarizes the conclusions and outlines directions for future work.

2 Problem Definition

The goal is to improve the extraction of spatial information from text by incorporating anaphora resolution for landmark candidates. We briefly define the spatial role labeling (SpRL) task which is based on a previous formalization of (Kordjamshidi et al., 2017b, 2011; Kordjamshidi and Moens, 2015b). Given a sentence S, segmented into phrases $P = [P_1, P_2, P_3, ...P_n]$ where P_i is the identifier of ith phrase in the sentence, the goal of spatial role labeling is to find the phrases which carry spatial roles (i.e. trajector (Tr), spatial indicator (Sp), landmark (Lm)), as introduced in Section 1 and identify the links between them to form spatial realtion, $R = [Tr, Sp, Lm]$. Moreover, each Spatial relation is further classified into coarse-grained type - (*region, direction, distance*) and fine-grained types based on their coarse-grained types (e.g. *(region,EC), (region,DC), (direction,left), (direction,right))*.

Figure 2 shows an example of spatial roles, spatial relations and spatial relation type extracted from a given text. In this example, the location of *statue (trajector)* is described with respect to the *hill (landmark)* using the preposition *on (spatial indicator)*. In Figure 1, the caption shows the textual description of an image, featuring multiple spatial relations ($\langle R_1 \leftarrow$[*a green*

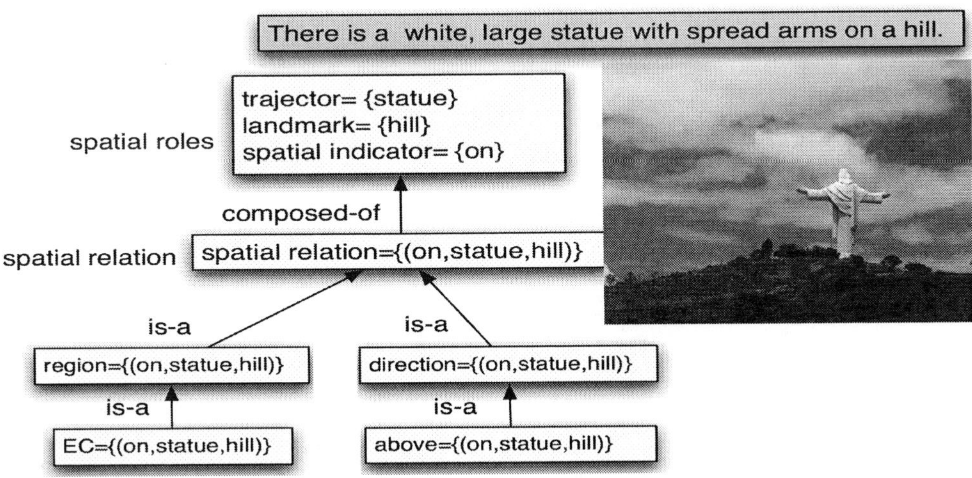

Figure 2: An Example of Spatial Roles and Relation Types.

$house]_{tr}$, $[among]_{sp}$, $[them]_{lm}\rangle$, $\langle R_2 \leftarrow [a\ white\ car]_{tr}$, $[in\ front\ of]_{sp}$, $[it]_{lm}\rangle$, $\langle R_3 \leftarrow [a\ blue-and-white\ church]_{tr}$, $[on\ the\ right]_{sp}$, $[None]_{lm}\rangle$ and $\langle R_4 \leftarrow [colorful\ houses]_{tr}$, $[on]_{sp}$, $[both\ sides]_{lm}\rangle)$ where R_1, R_2 have pronoun landmark, and R_3, R_4 have implicit landmarks (i.e. not mentioned in the given sentence). $R_1 \rightarrow$ landmark ($[it]_{lm}$), and $R_2 \rightarrow$ landmark ($[them]_{lm}$) are referring to $[colorful\ houses]$, and $[a\ green\ house]$ respectively. R_1, R_2 belongs to a well known anaphora resolution problem where the given pronoun is interpreted with the help of earlier or later items in the discourse whereas R_3, R_4 belongs to co-reference resolution problem (Lee et al., 2017b; Ng, 2010; Martschat and Strube, 2015) that aims at finding all expressions in the document that refer to the same entity.

The hypothesis of this paper is that how anaphora resolution for landmark candidates might help the inference for the extraction of roles as well as the relations from sentences. In this work, we proposed a model to address anaphora resolution for landmark candidates with the aim of improving the spatial relation extraction. In this paper, we assume that the antecedent (if any) of the anaphora (landmark here) is mentioned within the same sentence, therefore, cross-sentence anaphora resolution is not performed in this work.

3   Architecture

Depending on the description of the sentence, the spatial relations can contain pronoun land-marks (such as "it", "them", "him", "her"). Consider the aforementioned spatial relations R_1 and R_2 extracted from sentence T, $R_1 \rightarrow$ landmark ($[them]_{lm}$) and $R_2 \rightarrow$ landmark ($[it]_{lm}$) are referring to $[colorful\ houses]$ and $[a\ green\ house]$ phrases of the sentence T respectively. The components of computing the anaphora resolution for pronoun landmark spatial relations is described in the following subsections.

3.1   Exploiting External Knowledge

Given a candidate spatial relation R with a pronoun landmark, we are interested in finding the possible landmark objects which can occur with the given trajector and spatial indicator. For this purpose, we used an external resource, that is Visual Genome relationship dataset (VG). This dataset contains the relation (preposition) between various subjects and objects – for details see section 4.1. Given R, similar relations are extracted from visual genome dataset V by matching preposition and subject with $R \rightarrow spatialIndicator$ and $R \rightarrow trajector-headword$ respectively, that is the candidate words for the sp and tr roles.

In this way, we obtain the list of possible landmark objects and their frequencies in the VG dataset. We compute the frequency ratio per object and this ratio is interpreted as the possibility score of a relation containing that landmark. In other words, the score R_S is computed as $R_S \leftarrow O_{R_i}/T_{V_R}$ where O_{R_i} is the frequency of having object i with the given trajector-spatial indicator pair, and T_{V_R} is the

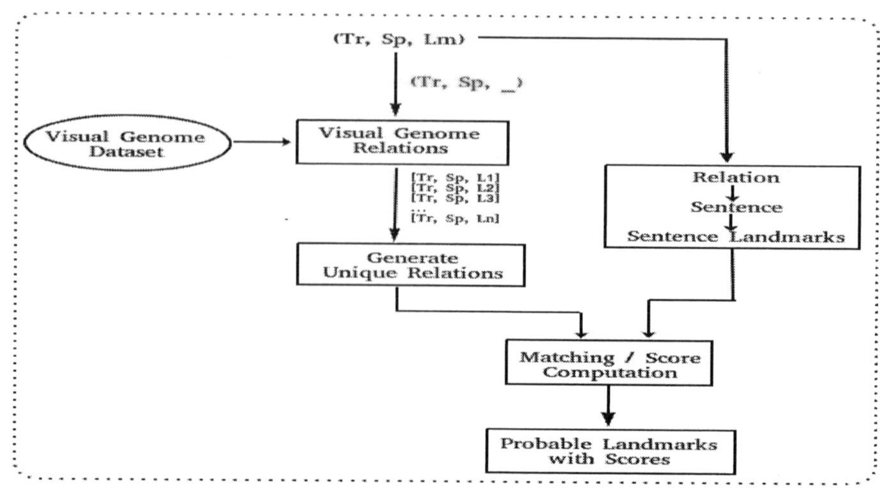

Figure 3: Probable landmark extraction model

total relations frequency for given trajector-spatial indicator pair in VG dataset. This will yield the set of possible triplets given the trajector-indicator pair with a score assigned to each triplet. We denote this set as, $U_R = [(U_{R_1}, S_{U_{R_1}}), (U_{R_2}, S_{U_{R_2}}), ..., (U_{R_n}, S_{U_{R_n}})]$ where U_{R_i} and $S_{U_{R_i}}$ is the ith unique relation and its score respectively.

3.2 Scoring Landmark Candidate Resolvants

For each sentence we perform a pre-processing step based on the previous works and obtain a set of noun phrases that serve as the landmark candidates denoted by S_L. The aforementioned retrieved triplets from visual genome, U_R, can contain many landmarks which don't exist in our landmarks candidates set, therefore, in this step, we compute the similarity (using Google Word2Vec) score between each landmark in S_L with all U_R landmarks. The final score for each candidate landmark in the sentence will be the maximum score that is computed by averaging the similarity score and occurrence score of that landmark with respect to all U_R candidates. In this way we obtain a score for each candidate landmark in S_L.

3.3 Learning Model

We formulate this problem as a structured output prediction problem where given a set of input-output pairs as training examples, $E = \{(x^i, y^i) \in \mathcal{X} \times \mathcal{Y} : i = 1..N\}$, an objective function $g(x, y; W) = \langle W, f(x, y) \rangle$ is learned. This function is a linear discriminant function defined over combined feature representation of inputs and outputs denoted by $f(x, y)$. However, in this work,

independent classifiers are trained per role and relations and only the predication is performed based on the global inference as in (Kordjamshidi et al., 2017a; Rahgooy et al., 2018).

We construct a graph using the phrases $\{p_1, ..., p_n\}$ (i.e. each phrase is a node in the graph) and link these nodes to make composed concepts such as relations. A classifier is associated with each concept in the graph and the domain knowledge is encoded over these concepts by global constraints. Global reasoning is imposed over these classifiers to produce the final outputs by using these constraints. Furthermore, we used binary classifiers to classify the spatial roles and relations where trajector, landmark, spatial indicator are denoted by tr, sp, lm respectively and $sp.tr.lm$, $sp.tr.lm.\gamma$, $sp.tr.lm.\lambda$ denotes spatial relations, coarse-grained relations, and fine-grained relations. Additionally, we denote the *new-relation-classifier* described in section 3.5 by $sp.tr.lm_{NRC}$.

Each phrase in the sentence is described by a vector of linguistic features denoted by: $\psi_{phrase}(p_i)$ (e.g. word form, POS tag, headword POS tag, dependencyRelation, subCategorization, etc), these features are used by spatial role classifiers. The spatial relation is composed of three phrases (p_i, p_j, p_k), therefore, the combination of these phrases along with their descriptive vectors are used in the spatial relation feature set referred as: $\phi_{triplet}^{text}(p_i, p_j, p_k)$ (e.g. distance between trajector and spatial indicator, concatenation of trajector, spatial indicator, and landmark). These features are proposed by (Roberts and Harabagiu, 2012) and (Kordjamshidi et al., 2017a).

56

1	$\sum_i \sum_k sp_i tr_j lm_k \geq tr_j$	Each tr candidate at least should appear in one relation
2	$\sum_i \sum_j sp_i tr_j lm_k \geq lm_k$	Each lm candidate at least should appear in one relation
3	$\sum_j \sum_k sp_i tr_j lm_k = sp_i$	Each sp candidate should appear in one relation
4	$\sum_j tr_j \geq sp_i$	For each sp we should have at-least one tr
5	$\sum_k lm_k \geq sp_i$	For each sp we should have at-least one lm
6	$sp_i tr_j lm_k \gamma \leq sp_i tr_j lm_k$	is-a constraints between relations and coarse-grained types
7	$sp_i tr_j lm_k \lambda \leq sp_i tr_j lm_k \gamma$ $\lambda \in \Lambda_\gamma$	is-a constraints between coarse-grained and corresponding fine-grained types where Λ_γ denotes the candidate fine-grained types related to coarse-grained type γ.
8	$sp_i tr_j lm_{k_{NRC}} \leq sp_i tr_j lm_k$	Spatial relation with pronoun candidate should be classified as true if anyone in top N of the anaphora-resolved triplets is classified as true.

Table 1: Model Constraints.

3.4 Constraints

The global constraints used in our proposed model is combination of previously proposed constraints (1-7) (Rahgooy et al., 2018) and new one (constraint 8) described in Table 3.3. In fact, the global inference is performed using integer linear programming techniques subject to these constraints.

3.5 Global Prediction Model

We obtain the output of each classifier in the model holistically by global reasoning that is by considering global correlations among classifiers, when calculating outputs. This goal is achieved by optimizing an objective function that is the summation of classifiers' discriminant functions. The global objective function for our model is on the basis of our previous work as follows,

$$\sum_{i \in C_{sp}} \langle W_{sp}, \phi_{sp_i} \rangle . sp_i + \sum_{i \in C_{tr}} \langle W_{tr}, \phi_{tr_i} \rangle . tr_i +$$

$$\sum_{i \in C_{lm}} \langle W_{lm}, \phi_{lm_i} \rangle . lm_i +$$

$$\sum_{i \in C_{sp}} \sum_{j \in C_{tr}} \sum_{k \in C_{lm}} \langle W_{sptrlm}, \phi_{sp_i tr_j lm_k} \rangle . sp_i tr_j lm_k +$$

$$\sum_{\gamma \in \Gamma} \sum_{i \in C_{sp}} \sum_{j \in C_{tr}} \sum_{k \in C_{lm}} \langle W_{sptrlm}, \phi_{sp_i tr_j lm_k \gamma} \rangle . sp_i tr_j lm_k \gamma +$$

$$\sum_{\lambda \in \Lambda} \sum_{i \in C_{sp}} \sum_{j \in C_{tr}} \sum_{k \in C_{lm}} \langle W_{sptrlm}, \phi_{sp_i tr_j lm_k \lambda} \rangle . sp_i tr_j lm_k \lambda +$$

$$\sum_{\tau \in \Upsilon} \sum_{i \in C_{sp}} \sum_{j \in C_{tr}} \sum_{k \in C_{lm}} \langle W_{sptrlm}, \phi_{sp_i tr_j lm_{k_{NRC_\tau}}} \rangle . sp_i tr_j lm_{k_{NRC}}.$$

Each classifier is shown as a binary variable and Λ, Γ, Υ are the candidates for fine-grained relations, coarse-grained relations, and pronoun-landmark spatial relations respectively. The following model variations are designed to evaluate the performance of the proposed model. Furthermore, in all model variations, the CLEF 2017 mSprl dataset described in 4.1 is used for the training and evaluation of the classifiers.

- **Anaphora-Replacement** (A-Replacement): In this model, we replace the landmark phrase text of spatial relation where the landmark is a pronoun with the highest scored probable landmark (see 3.2), this approach is used for both training and testing. Furthermore, we train independent classifiers for spatial roles and relations classification. This is a learning only model where each classifier makes independent predictions. This model doesn't use any constraints, and is compared with similar (Rahgooy et al., 2018) baseline model in section 4.

- **Anaphora-Inference** (A-Inference): In this model, 1) we create an additional triplet classifier for classifying the relations that contain pronoun landmarks and we name it *new-relation-classifier (NRC)* and use it at the inference time, 2) joint prediction is performed using the constraints described in

	A-Replacement			M0		
	Precision	Recall	F1	Precision	Recall	F1
$Trajector$	53.24	67.66	59.59	54.22	62.05	57.87
$Landmark$	73.49	81.23	77.17	74.29	78.60	76.38
$SpatialIndicator$	94.60	96.98	95.78	94.60	96.98	95.78

Table 2: Spatial Roles - Comparison of A-Replacement with M0

	A-Inference			M0+C		
	Precision	Recall	F1	Precision	Recall	F1
$Trajector$	65.79	65.39	65.59	64.20	60.98	62.55
$Landmark$	84.69	78.60	81.53	79.09	82.28	80.65
$SpatialIndicator$	94.70	96.60	95.64	95.08	94.84	94.96

Table 3: Spatial Roles - Comparison of A-Inference with M0+C

3.4 to optimize the global objective function explained in section 3.5 which includes the *new-relation-classifier*. This implies that both relation classifier and the *new-relation-classifier* are assigned values jointly and should agree. For training the *new-relation-classifier*, we generate additional examples by replacing the pronoun landmarks in the ground-truth with the highest scored landmark from our candidate set, S_L. The original spatial relations with pronoun landmarks are also retained in the training. The training mechanism of remaining classifiers remains unchanged (i.e. trained on original spatial relations). In testing phase, we take the top N candidates from the scored landmarks generated in 3.2 for spatial relations with pronoun landmarks. In this way, we regenerate a set of candidate triplets by replacing the pronoun with the top probable landmarks. Our global inference decides jointly with using the original triplet classifier in a way that it satisfies the constraint that if anyone of these triplets is predicted as true, spatial relation classifier is forced at inference time to predict the spatial relation with the anaphora as true. See constraint number 8 in section 3.4. The experiments show that this simple idea can promote the relation extraction when anaphora occurs in the triplet candidates.

4 Experiments

4.1 Datasets

CLEF 2017 mSpRL dataset: Our model is evaluated on this dataset which is a subset of IAPR TC-12[1] Benchmark and annotated specifically for the SpRL task. The training set contains 761 and whereas test set contains 939 spatial relations respectively (Kordjamshidi et al., 2017b). The total number of spatial relations containing pronoun landmark in train and test is 44 and 129 respectively.

Visual Genome dataset (VG): Visual Genome dataset has seven main components (Krishna et al., 2017), one of it is 'relationships' which contains the relationships between pairs of objects in the images. Each relation has two arguments, the first one is referred as subject whereas the latter one is referred as object. These relationships can be actions, spatial, prepositions, verbs, comparative or prepositional phrases. Visual genome dataset contains 108077 images whereas its relationships part contains 2316104 relation instances. This dataset is used to obtain the possible landmarks that can occur in a relationship with a given subject.

4.2 Experimental Results

In this section, we experimentally show the effectiveness of our proposed model in improving the spatial role/relation extraction. We use *Saul* (Kordjamshidi et al., 2015, 2016) to implement models and solve the global inference of Section 3.5. The code is publicly available here[2].

We compare our approach with the state-of-the-art (Rahgooy et al., 2018). However, in the mentioned paper, the authors use visual data from the accompanying images to improve the models. In

---

[1]http://www.imageclef.org/SIAPRdata
[2]https://github.com/HetML/SpRL/tree/paper3

	Precision	Recall	F1
$M0$	65.64	60.23	62.82
$M0 + C$	70.04	66.55	68.25
$A\text{-}Replacement$	78.47	56.84	65.92
$A\text{-}Inference$	70.23	68.25	69.23

Table 4: Model Comparison - Spatial Relation Extraction

	A-Replacement			M0		
	Precision	Recall	F1	Precision	Recall	F1
$Region$	70.90	54.24	61.52	78.37	47.83	59.41
$Direction$	79.22	43.57	56.22	83.56	43.57	57.28

Table 5: Coarse-grained Spatial Relations - Comparison of A-Replacement with M0.

this paper, we use their best model (referred here as $M0$ -Baseline and $M0 + C$ -Baseline plus constraints) which is trained on text only and we ignore the visual information which is aligned with the text. The experimental results in Table 4 show that our baseline model (A-Replacement) is significantly better as compared to the state-of-the-art baseline model (M0). This shows that replacing the pronoun landmark candidates with our proposed model probable landmark has positive impact on extraction of spatial roles (as shown in Table 2) and relations. The improvement in the results is because the spatial roles predication is improved, which gives a more confidence to the model to classify the triplets as spatial relations which leads to more positive predictions and higher recall of the relations.

Furthermore, our second model (A-Inference) in which we train an additional *new-relation-classifier* by generating additional examples and perform joint inference further improves the results over the state-of-the-art model with constraints (M0+C). The experimental results in Table 3 show that adding constraints to our second model (A+Inference) significantly improves the classification of spatial roles (i.e. trajectors and landmarks), although the spatial indicators is slightly improved. Also these constraints help improving the coarse-grained spatial relations as shown in table 6, although it doesn't have any impact on distance category because the number of examples in test set is very small (i.e. three instances only).

Our results improve the state-of-the-art models for spatial relation extraction. Both proposed models significantly improves the extraction of spatial roles and relations (when compared with independent learning and with constrained models). However, the results of some of the categories in the fine-grained relations drops which are not reported here. These results are at the preliminary stage and we further analyze our models. Particularly, we will use existing anaphora resolution models to see how those could help and provide a more reasonable baseline. This baseline will help us to evaluate the advantage of the external visual knowledge more clearly. It will be interesting to investigate what caused this drop in fine-grained relation types. In addition to such further analysis, this work can be extended into two possible directions, 1) incorporate cross-sentence anaphora resolution for landmark candidates, and 2) incorporate co-reference resolution in general for all spatial relations.

5   Related Work

Our proposed model is a joint model for considering anaphora resolution to help spatial information extraction. Anaphora resolution is a fundamental problem in natural language processing and existing techniques can broadly be categorized into two types 1) Rule based models: apply rules to reduce candidate antecedents and resolve anaphora and 2) statistical models: use probabilistic models for the resolution of anaphora (Lee et al., 2017a). Early work (Hobbs, 1978; Asher and Wada, 1988; Lappin and Leass, 1994; Morton, 2000) focused on designing rule-based systems for anaphora resolution (the target was finding antecedents of pronouns only), however, these systems relied heavily on handcraft rules/weights. In early 2000, (Soon et al., 2001; Yang et al., 2003; Ng and Cardie, 2002) used statistical machine learning methods to resolve co-reference, these methods used a com-

	A-Inference			M0+C		
	Precision	Recall	F1	Precision	Recall	F1
Region	72.99	60.82	66.35	76.07	57.79	65.68
Direction	76.26	46.67	57.90	75.75	48.33	59.01

Table 6: Coarse-grained Spatial Relations - Comparison of A-Inference with M0+C.

mon strategy, that is, train a statistical model to measure the likeness of a pair as corefer. However, each candidate is resolved independently of the others which means how good a candidate antecedent is relative to others is not considered. To address this problem, (Denis and Baldridge, 2009) proposed a model by combining machine learning with global inference for performing the resolution jointly. Recently, (Park et al., 2016) proposed an mention pair model using deep learning and a system that combines both rule-based and deep learning-based systems using a guided MP model for co-reference resolution.

According to (Lee et al., 2017a), machine learning based models for anaphora resolution are relatively easy to build as compared to rule based models, however, a huge amount of handcrafted feature design is required in order to build a successful anaphora resolution model. Furthermore, the authors highlighted four key features of a ideal anaphora resolution system one of which is antecedent features should be learned automatically (i.e. minimum human design effort should be required). The proposed model doesn't require any handcrafting features or rules to implement the anaphora resolvers.

Join models have been proposed for resolving co-references with mention head detection using underlying integer linear programming as we do here (Peng et al., 2015). The main difference of our work compared to the above mentioned research works is that here we do not directly solve the anaphora resolution problem, but we use a kind of indirect supervision from an external multi-modal resource to help anaphora resolution and by means of that we solve our specific target problem. Our target problem of spatial information extraction has not been jointly performed with neither anaphora nor co-reference resolution tasks before. However, resolving co-references in the multi-modal setting has been investigated recently (Huang et al., 2017) in which text and video refer to the same scene and help each other in the resolution. As pointed above, this is different from using the vision modality as a source of distant supervision which is our aim in this work.

6 Conclusion

In this paper, we investigated the challenging issues of the extraction of spatial relations, that is, the triplets of (spatial indicator, trajector, landmark) from generic text. Particularly, We highlighted one important problem that is the issue of anaphoras accruing in the text that make recognizing landmarks and consequently recognizing the spatial relations difficult. In the presence of the anaphora recognizing the right link between the described objects in the text and extracting the relations correctly for any arbitrary pair of object becomes more challenging. Our proposed solution has been to use the external visual resources that can help to find out the most probable landmarks for a specific object and obtain the possible resolutions with a score. Using the scored resolutions we perform global inference to decide on both the anaphora resolution and spatial relation extraction jointly. Our best model improves the state-of-the-art results in all precision, recall and F1 metrics while having a more positive (about +2%) influence on the recall of the spatial relations extraction. While our preliminary experimental results show the advantage of anaphora resolution in spatial relation extraction, we will investigate more sophisticated baselines in the future to evaluate the advantage of external knowledge resources (that we used in this work) versus using the existing approaches for anaphora resolution in our models.

References

Nicholas Asher and Hajime Wada. 1988. A computational account of syntactic, semantic and discourse principles for anaphora resolution. *Journal of Semantics*, 6(1):309–344.

Pascal Denis and Jason Baldridge. 2009. Global joint models for coreference resolution and named entity classification. *Procesamiento del Lenguaje Natural*, 42.

Jennifer D'Souza and Vincent Ng. 2015. Sieve-based spatial relation extraction with expanding parse trees. In *Proceedings of the 2015 Conference on Empirical Methods in Natural Language Processing*, pages 758–768.

Jerry R. Hobbs. 1978. Resolving pronoun references. *Lingua*, 44(4):311 – 338.

De-An Huang, Joseph J. Lim, Fei-Fei Li, and Juan Carlos Niebles. 2017. Unsupervised visual-linguistic reference resolution in instructional videos. *CoRR*, abs/1703.02521.

P. Kordjamshidi, D. Roth, and H. Wu. 2015. Saul: Towards declarative learning based programming. In *Proc. of the International Joint Conference on Artificial Intelligence (IJCAI)*.

Parisa Kordjamshidi, Daniel Khashabi, Christos Christodoulopoulos, Bhargav Mangipudi, Sameer Singh, and Dan Roth. 2016. Better call saul: Flexible programming for learning and inference in nlp. In *Proceedings of COLING 2016, the 26th International Conference on Computational Linguistics: Technical Papers*, pages 3030–3040.

Parisa Kordjamshidi and Marie-Francine Moens. 2015a. Global machine learning for spatial ontology population. *Web Semantics: Science, Services and Agents on the World Wide Web*, 30:3–21.

Parisa Kordjamshidi and Marie-Francine Moens. 2015b. Global machine learning for spatial ontology population. *Web Semant.*, 30(C):3–21.

Parisa Kordjamshidi, Taher Rahgooy, and Umar Manzoor. 2017a. Spatial language understanding with multimodal graphs using declarative learning based programming. In *Proceedings of the 2nd Workshop on Structured Prediction for Natural Language Processing*, pages 33–43.

Parisa Kordjamshidi, Taher Rahgooy, Marie-Francine Moens, James Pustejovsky, Umar Manzoor, and Kirk Roberts. 2017b. Clef 2017: Multimodal spatial role labeling (msprl) task overview. In *International Conference of the Cross-Language Evaluation Forum for European Languages*, pages 367–376. Springer.

Parisa Kordjamshidi, Martijn van Otterlo, and Marie-Francine Moens. 2011. Spatial role labeling: towards extraction of spatial relations from natural language. *ACM - Transactions on Speech and Language Processing*, 8:1–36.

Ranjay Krishna, Yuke Zhu, Oliver Groth, Justin Johnson, Kenji Hata, Joshua Kravitz, Stephanie Chen, Yannis Kalantidis, Li-Jia Li, David A Shamma, et al. 2017. Visual genome: Connecting language and vision using crowdsourced dense image annotations. *International Journal of Computer Vision*, 123(1):32–73.

Shalom Lappin and Herbert J. Leass. 1994. An algorithm for pronominal anaphora resolution. *Comput. Linguist.*, 20(4):535–561.

Changki Lee, Sangkeun Jung, and Cheon-Eum Park. 2017a. Anaphora resolution with pointer networks. *Pattern Recognition Letters*, 95:1 – 7.

Kenton Lee, Luheng He, Mike Lewis, and Luke Zettlemoyer. 2017b. End-to-end neural coreference resolution. *CoRR*, abs/1707.07045.

Ana Marasovic, Leo Born, Juri Opitz, and Anette Frank. 2017. A mention-ranking model for abstract anaphora resolution. *CoRR*, abs/1706.02256.

Sebastian Martschat and Michael Strube. 2015. Latent structures for coreference resolution. *TACL*, 3:405–418.

Ruslan Mitkov. 2005. *The Oxford Handbook of Computational Linguistics (Oxford Handbooks)*. Oxford University Press, Inc., New York, NY, USA.

Ruslan Mitkov, Richard Evans, Constantin Orăsan, Le An Ha, and Viktor Pekar. 2007. Anaphora resolution: To what extent does it help nlp applications? In *Proceedings of the 6th Discourse Anaphora and Anaphor Resolution Conference on Anaphora: Analysis, Algorithms and Applications*, DAARC'07, pages 179–190, Berlin, Heidelberg. Springer-Verlag.

Thomas S. Morton. 2000. Coreference for nlp applications. In *Proceedings of the 38th Annual Meeting on Association for Computational Linguistics*, ACL '00, pages 173–180, Stroudsburg, PA, USA. Association for Computational Linguistics.

Vincent Ng. 2010. Supervised noun phrase coreference research: The first fifteen years. In *Proceedings of the 48th Annual Meeting of the Association for Computational Linguistics*, ACL '10, pages 1396–1411, Stroudsburg, PA, USA. Association for Computational Linguistics.

Vincent Ng and Claire Cardie. 2002. Improving machine learning approaches to coreference resolution. In *Proceedings of the 40th Annual Meeting on Association for Computational Linguistics*, ACL '02, pages 104–111, Stroudsburg, PA, USA. Association for Computational Linguistics.

Cheoneum Park, Kyoung-Ho Choi, Changki Lee, and Soojong Lim. 2016. Korean coreference resolution with guided mention pair model using deep learning. *ETRI Journal*, 38(6):1207–1217.

Haoruo Peng, Kai-Wei Chang, and Dan Roth. 2015. A joint framework for coreference resolution and mention head detection. In *CoNLL*.

James Pustejovsky, Parisa Kordjamshidi, Marie-Francine Moens, Aaron Levine, Seth Dworman, and Zachary Yocum. 2015. Semeval-2015 task 8: Spaceeval. In *Proc. of the Annual Meeting of the*

Association for Computational Linguistics (ACL), pages 884–894. ACL.

Taher Rahgooy, Umar Manzoor, and Parisa Kordjamshidi. 2018. Visually guided spatial relation extraction from text. In *Proceedings of the 2018 Conference of the North American Chapter of the Association for Computational Linguistics on Human Language Technology*. Association for Computational Linguistics.

Kirk Roberts and Sanda M Harabagiu. 2012. Utd-sprl: A joint approach to spatial role labeling. In *Proceedings of the First Joint Conference on Lexical and Computational Semantics-Volume 1: Proceedings of the main conference and the shared task, and Volume 2: Proceedings of the Sixth International Workshop on Semantic Evaluation*, pages 419–424. Association for Computational Linguistics.

Wee Meng Soon, Hwee Tou Ng, and Daniel Chung Yong Lim. 2001. A machine learning approach to coreference resolution of noun phrases. *Computational Linguistics*, 27(4):521–544.

Xiaofeng Yang, Guodong Zhou, Jian Su, and Chew Lim Tan. 2003. Coreference resolution using competition learning approach. In *Proceedings of the 41st Annual Meeting on Association for Computational Linguistics - Volume 1*, ACL '03, pages 176–183, Stroudsburg, PA, USA. Association for Computational Linguistics.

The Case for Systematically Derived Spatial Language Usage

Bonnie Dorr
Institute for Human and Machine Cognition
15 SE Osceola Ave, Ocala, FL 34471
bdorr@ihmc.us

Clare Voss
U.S. Army Research Laboratory
Adelphi, MD 20783
clare.r.voss.civ@mail.mil

Abstract

This position paper argues that, while prior work in spatial language understanding for tasks such as robot navigation focuses on mapping natural language into deep conceptual or non-linguistic representations, it is possible to systematically derive regular patterns of spatial language usage from existing lexical-semantic resources. Furthermore, even with access to such resources, effective solutions to many application areas such as robot navigation and narrative generation also require additional knowledge at the syntax-semantics interface to cover the wide range of spatial expressions observed and available to natural language speakers. We ground our insights in, and present our extensions to, an existing lexico-semantic resource, covering 500 semantic classes of verbs, of which 219 fall within a spatial subset. We demonstrate that these extensions enable systematic derivation of regular patterns of spatial language without requiring manual annotation.

1 Introduction

While prior work in spatial language understanding for tasks such as robot navigation focuses on mapping natural language into deep conceptual or non-linguistic representations—for further reasoning or embodied cognition (Perera et al., 2017; Pastra et al., 2011)—we argue that it is possible to systematically derive regular patterns of language usage from existing lexical-semantic resources (Dorr et al., 2001). Furthermore, even with access to such resources, effective solutions to many application areas such as robot navigation and narrative generation require additional knowledge at the syntax-semantics interface to capture the range of spatial expressions observed and available to natural language speakers.

The emphasis of this position paper is on the representational underpinnings of spatial expressions for problems such as natural-language mediated two-way human-robot dialogue. Such communication may ultimately take place over low bandwidth networks where, for example, an autonomous robot will navigate and report back from a remote site on what it sees in cooperation with its distant human teammate who directs and responds to the robot as needed. We focus on the use and modification of existing resources to address this problem, making certain linguistically-motivated, working assumptions about:

- layers within our lexical representations,
- levels for distinct language-based modules with syntactic, semantic, and conceptual knowledge (each with primitives and operations for that level), and
- a shared computational model of an environment that includes representations of objects, agents, their relations to each other, events—thus enabling navigation information to be accessible to both robot and human.

That is, we assume first that there exist lexical-internal semantic structures with layers, and those semantic structures contain primitives that are grounded at a conceptual level (not discussed herein). We leverage Lexical Conceptual Structure (LCS) (Jackendoff, 1983; Dorr, 1993), a logical representation with compositional properties, to guide development of semantics for spatial language in language understanding and generation.[1]

We note that other logical representations may also be adequate for this study, e.g., Abstract Meaning Representation (Banarescu et al., 2014), Prague Dependency Trees (Hajič et al., 2018), and descendants of such representations (Vanderwende et al., 2015). LCS has been selected due

---

[1] We take these structures to capture language-bound meanings, that is semantic forms. In our framework, these do not, despite their name, capture language-independent, conceptual knowledge.

Proceedings of the First International Workshop on Spatial Language Understanding (SpLU-2018), pages 63–70
New Orleans, Louisiana, June 6, 2018. ©2018 Association for Computational Linguistics

to its compositional, lexicon-based formalism and its potential for follow-on work in other language processing applications for which cross-lingual LCS mappings have already been devised (e.g., machine translation (Habash and Dorr, 2002)).

We assume second, that for human-robot natural-language mediated communication, a number of constraints at the syntax-semantics interface are crucial for interpreting the wide ranging flexibility of real utterances and the context of the system is central to dialogue management. We leverage previously collected dialogue data with naturally occurring spoken Bot Language (Marge et al., 2017) that provides transcripts and dialog analyses (Traum et al., 2018), but without any form of lexical semantics.

We assume third, that we will test and validate our approach by augmenting an implemented dialogue system for understanding and generation of Bot Language. The application of our foundational paradigm to this problem is a future direction outside of the scope of this position paper.

The layered lexical representations referred to in the first assumption above form the basis for this discussion. Specifically, we posit that the development of an application such as robot navigation (Bonial et al., 2018; Moolchandani et al., 2018) or generation of narrative explanations (Korpan et al., 2017; Lukin et al., 2018) requires a layered representation scheme to include a set of spatial primitives (the basis for the LCS representation) coupled with a representation of constraints at the syntax-semantics interface. Additional layers include prepositional collocates[2] and spatial semantics that are crucial for understanding and production of unconstrained spatial expressions.

We describe our extensions to an LCS resource covering 500 semantic classes of verbs, of which 219 fall within a spatial subset. We demonstrate that this resource is designed to systematically account for certain types of spatial expressions based on lexical-semantic constraints of spatial verbs in those expressions.

At the heart of the position presented herein is a representational framework that supports the ability to "read off" such constraints from lexical entries without requiring laborious manual annota-

tion. Similarly, when subsequent lexicon updates occur, the ability to "read off" constraints is still available without manual annotation. This differentiates our approach from others, e.g., feature-based annotation (for a cogent review of natural language annotation approaches, see (Stubbs and Pustejovsky, 2012)). Our LCS-based approach is described next, followed by related work and concluding remarks.

2 Approach

This section introduces the notion of LCS and describes an LCS-based approach to systematic derivation of usage patterns for understanding and generation. We extend an LCS resource to include constraints (blocks, overlaps, and fills) and present the upshot of these extensions.

2.1 Lexical Conceptual Structure

Lexical Conceptual Structure (LCS) (Jackendoff, 1983, 1990; Dorr, 1993; Dowty, 1979; Guerssel et al., 1985) has been used for a range of different applications, including interlingual machine translation (Habash and Dorr, 2002), lexical acquisition (Habash et al., 2006), cross-language information retrieval (Levow et al., 2000), language generation (Traum and Habash, 2000), and intelligent language tutoring (Dorr, 1997).

The LCS representation was introduced by Jackendoff as based in the spatial domain and naturally extended to non-spatial domains, as specified by *fields*.[3] For example, the spatial dimension of the LCS representation corresponds to the *(Loc)ational* field, which underlies the meaning of *John traveled from Chicago to Boston* in the LCS [John GO$_{Loc}$ [From Chicago] [To Boston]]. This is straightforwardly extended to the *(Temp)oral* field to represent analogous meanings such as *The meeting went from 7pm to 9pm* in the LCS [Meeting GO$_{Temp}$ [From 7pm] [To 9pm]].

An "LCS Verb Database" (LVD) developed in prior work (Dorr et al., 2001) includes a set of LCS templates classified according to an extension of (Levin, 1993)'s 192 classes, totaling 500 classes. The first 44 classes were added beyond the original set of semantic classes (Dorr and Jones, 1996). Additional classes were derived through aspectual distinctions to yield *LCS classes* that were finer-grained than the original Levin classes (Olsen

---

[2]Prepositions that, when tested in collocations with otherwise non-spatial expressions, add spatial information. For example, in *The hawk screeched across the sky.*, the prepositional phrase headed by *across* introduces motion not present in the intransitive *The hawk screeched* (Talmy, 2014).

[3]For a more extensive, non-LCS-based analysis and accounting of the relation of spatial and temporal concepts, see (Tenbrink, 2011).

et al., 1997). Each LCS class consists of a set of verbs and, in several cases, the classes include *non-Levin words* (those not in (Levin, 1993)), derived semi-automatically (Dorr, 1997). LVD is foundational for the position adopted in this paper, as it provides a mapping from LCS-based verb classes to their surface realizations.

The representational framework provided by the LVD has many similarities with others such as FrameNet (Ruppenhofer et al., 2016) and Verb-Net (Palmer et al., 2017), both of which also include classes and mappings to surface realizations. Whereas FrameNet has a richer semantics, e.g., finer grained classes than those of Levin (1993), VerbNet has a clearer mapping to surface realizations with specific mappings from thematic roles to syntactic realizations.The LVD differs from both of these in that its compositional representations support the ability to "read off"different types of lexical-semantic constraints without requiring manual annotation. For example, constraints on the mapping between semantics and syntax, e.g., blocks, overlaps, and fills, can be "read off" LVD entries, as described below.

2.2 Syntax-Semantics Interface

Prior work (Jackendoff, 1996; Levin, 1993; Dorr and Voss, 1993; Voss and Dorr, 1995; Kipper et al., 2007; Palmer et al., 2017) suggests that there is a close relation between underlying lexical-semantic structures of verbs and nominal predicates and their syntactic argument structure. The work of Voss et al. (1998) supports that the generation of a preposition (in English) as dependent on both the semantics of the predicate and structural idiosyncracies at the syntax-semantics interface.

Three notions introduced in this earlier work are relevant to spatial language understanding: BLOCK (where a LCS predicate preempts or blocks the composition into one of its argument positions by another LCS), OVERLAPS (where a LCS predicate allows the composition of another LCS into one of its already-occupied arguments), and FILLS (where a LCS predicate allows the composition of another correctly typed LCS into one of its empty arguments).

To investigate the systematic derivation of language usage patterns for both understanding and generation of spatial language, we first simplify and adapt the LVD to include mappings to both lexically implicit and lexically explicit directional components of meaning. We focus specifi-

Prepositional collocates: up, down, in, into, out of, across, to, from, etc..

Spatial Semantics: upward, downward, etc.

LCS Primitives: GO, BE, STAY, CAUSE, etc.

Blocks
Overlaps
Fills

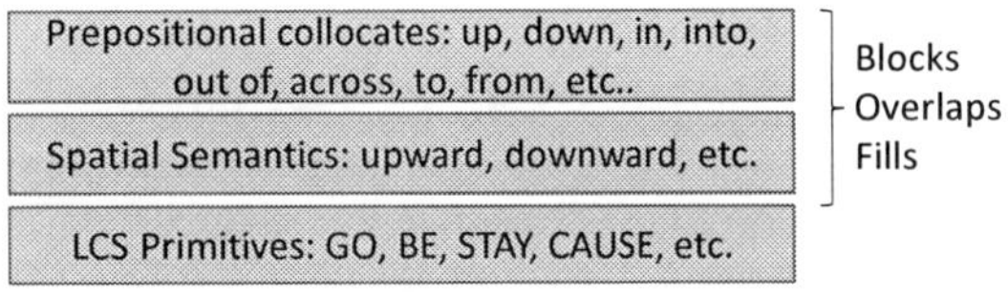

Figure 1: Layered Representation Scheme: Spatial primitives (bottom layer) are coupled with spatial semantics (middle layer) and spatial semantics (top layer) for spatial language understanding and generation

cally on directional verbs coupled with these implicit/explicit directional components of meaning.

We posit that the development of a framework for both understanding and generation of spatial language requires a layered representation scheme illustrated in Figure 1. The top two layers rely heavily on the notions of BLOCKS, OVERLAPS, and FILLS. More specifically:

- **BLOCKS** refers to *lexically implicit* directional components of meaning (such as `upward`) that cannot be lexically realized on the surface, as happens when a predicate already includes the corresponding directional component of meaning, e.g., *elevate* and *ascend* do not collocate with the preposition *up*.

- **OVERLAPS** refers to *lexically implicit and optionally explicit* directional components of meaning (such as `upward`) that may or may not be lexically realized on the surface even though the semantics of the predicate includes the corresponding directional component of meaning, e.g., *lift* and *raise* optionally collocate with *up*.

- **FILLS** refers to *lexically explicit* directional components of meanings that fall into one of two categories: (1) *obligatory* components of meaning (such as `upward`) that must be lexically realized, as the semantics of the predicate does not include the corresponding directional component of meaning, e.g., *put* always collocates with a preposition such as *up*. (2) *optional* components of meaning (such as `upward`) that may or may not be lexically realized, as the semantics of the predicate does not include directional component of meaning, e.g., *move* optionally collocates with a preposition, such as *up*.

The LVD described in Section 2.1 includes compositional structures based on primitives such as GO, BE, STAY, CAUSE. These structures, which form the foundation for the bottom layer, are outside of the scope of this paper.

2.3 Upshot of Lexico-Semantic Extensions for Spatial Language Understanding

An adapted form of the LVD has been developed for the purpose of illustrating the position taken in this paper. This derivative resource contains simplified LCS classes, omitting the full LCS structures and thematic roles from prior work, and augmenting LCS classes to include prepositional *collocations* (the top layer of Figure 1), coupled with a new *spatial component of meaning* (the middle layer of Figure 1).

The spatial component of meaning may or may not be overtly realized on the surface. For example, in the LCS Class of *Verbs of inherently directed motion* (corresponding to Class 51.1.a in (Levin, 1993)), the verb *leave* can take a NP complement (as in *leave the room*) and the verb *depart* can take a PP complement (as in *departed from the room*). For either case, the spatial component of meaning is uniformly `move to a position outside of the room`.

Whereas the collocations were derived from thematic roles in the original LVD, the spatial components of meaning were derived from verb-prepositions pairs associated with a subset of the "Categorial Variation" database (Habash and Dorr, 2003). Representative members of LCS classes were then paired with prepositions that were propagated to other members of the class.

Table 1 summarizes the number of LCS classes associated with the lexical notions introduced above (Blocks, Overlaps, Fills-Oblig, Fills-Opt).[4] Not all LCS classes are spatial in nature; thus, the second column provides a tally for the full set of LCS classes, and the third column provides a tally for just the spatial subset. The fourth column presents the number of spatial verbs included in the corresponding spatial classes. Representative spatial examples are provided in the fifth column.

Lexical Notions	LCS Classes	Spatial Subset	#Spatial verbs	Spatial Examples
Blocks	7	7	297	elevate, face, pocket
Overlaps	17	10	84	advance, lower, lift
Fills-Oblig	310	128	2783	drive, rotate, put
Fills-Opt	87	59	1280	remove, slide
Intrans	6	3	34	float, part, squirm
N/A	73	12	162	bend, break, carry
Total	500	219	4640	

Table 1: Summary of number of classes associated with Blocks, Overlaps, Fills-Oblig, Fills-Opt, and Intrans in LCS Classes and Spatial Subset

---

[4]N/A refers to verb classes whose members take bare NP or S arguments. Intrans refers to Intransitive verbs.

Interestingly, the spatial subset of classes is sizeable (44% of the entire set of 500 classes). The percentage of verb entries in the spatial subset is also quite high (42% of the 11K total number of verb entries). Several verbs in the Spatial Subset are relevant to those used in robot navigation, e.g., *move, go, advance, drive, return, rotate,* and *turn*. Others are easily accommodated by extending classes—without modification to the spatial notions described above. For example, *back up* matches the class containing *advance*, and *pivot* matches the class containing *rotate*.

Note that the BLOCKS, OVERLAPS, AND FILLS notions are generalizable to a high number of LCS classes that are non-spatial as well. These typically correspond to metaphorical extensions of spatial components of meaning to other domains, e.g., *lifted her spirits up, elevated her spirits*. Thus, these notions are more broadly applicable than just to the spatial dimension.

Ultimately, surface realizations of verbs with collocations include lexically explicit prepositions as in *lift up*, whereas no such collocates are available when spatial components of meaning are internally conveyed as in *elevate* and thus are lexically implicit. Adding this information to the derivative resource supports a refined formulation of BLOCKS, OVERLAPS, and FILLS notions– which are central to a range of important problems, e.g., dialogue management in robot navigation (Bonial et al., 2017) and generation of narrative explanations (Korpan et al., 2017).

3 Related Work

The ever-growing number of interdisciplinary research programs that now involve natural language processing but are published outside of computational linguistics, provides both challenges and opportunities to all communities seeking to leverage emerging insights from beyond their own areas of expertise. In this short position paper, we highlight but two areas pertinent to our work, while acknowledging there exists much other research in situated dialogue for robots (e.g., (Mavridis and Roy, 2006; Kruiff et al., 2007)) and spatial cognition (e.g., publications of the Spatial Cognition collaborative research center in Germany) that is not as central to our focus.

3.1 Spatial Language Understanding

Spatial language understanding has made great strides in recent years, with the emergence of language resources and standards for capturing spatial information. For example, the ISO 24617 standard provides guidelines for annotating spatial information in English language texts (24617-7, 2014) that continues to evolve (Pustejovsky and Lee, 2017). This Semantic Annotation Framework (semAF) identifies places, paths, spatial entities, and spatial relations that can be used to associate sequences of processes and events in news articles (Pustejovsky et al., 2011). Spatial prepositions and particles (such as *near, off*) and verbs of position and movement (such as *lean, swim*) in text have corresponding spatial components of meanings, collocations, and classes of spatial verbs in the perspective adopted in this paper.

Spatial role labeling using holistic spatial semantics (i.e., analysis at the level of the full utterance) has been used for identifying spatial relations between objects (Kordjamshidi et al., 2010). The association between thematic roles and their corresponding surface realizations has been investigated previously, including in the LCS formalism (described next), but Kordjamshidi et al's approach also ties into deeper notions such as *region of space* and *frame of reference*. Their work differs from the perspective adopted in this paper in that they provide annotation guidelines for training systems that do spatial information extraction, and so do not focus on generalized mappings at the syntax-semantics interface to predict possible linguistic constructs for spatial relations.

3.2 Embodied Cognition

Another research area relevant to the position adopted herein is that of embodied cognition for the development of language processing tools (Pastra et al., 2011). A European-funded project (POETICON) has resulted in a suite of embodied language processing tools relating symbolic and sensorimotor representation spaces. This work sheds light on the nature of the relationship between language and action, enabling exploration of a range of different projects concerning language learning and human-robot interaction.

Other researchers have focused on natural language grounding for embodied interaction (Al-Omari et al., 2017) to learn components of language and the meanings of each word. The acquired knowledge that emerges from this approach is used to parse commands involving previously unseen objects. Thus, that work assumes no prior knowledge of the structure of language; rather, word meanings are learned from scratch. In contrast, the perspective put forward in this paper is one in which this knowledge already exists and can be leveraged for support of both language understanding and generation.

The work of Spranger et al. (2016) is the closest to our perspective, particularly in its use of spatial relations such as *across* and *in front of*, both for hearing and for producing utterances for robot-robot communication. However, the position adopted here is one in which generalizations about language structure are assumed and available in natural language generation for both *use* ("lift up") and *suppression* ("elevate") of spatial prepositions in phrases containing motion and direction verbs, depending on the context.

4 Conclusions and Future Work

We have made a case for the systematic derivation of regular patterns of spatial language usage from an existing lexical semantic resource (LCS Verb Lexicon). We have focused on a refined formulation of BLOCKS, OVERLAPS, and FILLS, lexical-semantic notions that are central to problems dialogue management in robot navigation and generation of narrative explanations. We demonstrated that these extensions enable systematic derivation of regular patterns of spatial language without requiring manual annotation.

Future work motivated by the position set forth in this paper is investigation of systematic derivation of mappings at the syntax-semantics interface for other parts of speech involving access to a "Categorial Variation" database (CatVar) (Habash and Dorr, 2003) to map verbs in the LCS classes to their nominalized and adjectivalized forms. For example, the CatVar entry for *depart* includes the nominalized form *departure*, which takes a prepositional-phrase complement (e.g., *from the room*)—analogous to the verbal counterpart specified in the simplified LCS classes.

Another future direction is one where these generalized mappings are used in conjunction with data collected within an ongoing Bot Language project (Marge et al., 2017) to enable spatial language understanding in robot navigation. That project has heretofore focused on dialogue annotation (Traum et al., 2018) and has not yet incorporated deeper semantics necessary for automatically detecting incomplete, vague, or implicit navigation commands within dialogues in the spatial domain—issues addressed by our extensions.

Acknowledgments

We would like to acknowledge and thank three anonymous reviewers for their careful reading of our manuscript and their many insightful comments and constructive suggestions. This research is supported, in part by the Institute for Human and Machine Cognition, in part by the U.S. Army Research Laboratory, and in part by the Office of the Director of National Intelligence (ODNI) and the Intelligence Advanced Research Projects Activity (IARPA) via the Air Force Research Laboratory (AFRL) contract number FA875016C0114. The U.S. Government is authorized to reproduce and distribute reprints for Governmental purposes notwithstanding any copyright annotation thereon. Disclaimer: The views and conclusions contained herein are those of the authors and should not be interpreted as necessarily representing the official policies or endorsements, either expressed or implied, of ODNI, IARPA, AFRL, ARL, or the U.S. Government.

References

ISO 24617-7. 2014. Language Resource management Semantic Annotation Framework Part 7: Spatial information (ISOspace). https://www.iso.org/standard/60779.html.

Muhannad Al-Omari, Paul Duckworth, David C. Hogg, and Anthony G. Cohn. 2017. Natural Language Acquisition and Grounding for Embodied Robotic Systems. In *Proceedings of the Thirty-First AAAI Conference on Artificial Intelligence, February 4-9, 2017, San Francisco, California, USA.*. pages 4349–4356.

Laura Banarescu, Claire Bonial, Shu Cai, Madalina Georgescu, Kira Griffitt, Ulf Hermjakob, Kevin Knight, Philipp Koehn, Martha Palmer, and Nathan Schneider. 2014. Abstract Meaning Representation (AMR) 1.2.1 Specification. https://github.com/amrisi/amrguidelines/blob/master/amr.md.

Claire Bonial, Stephanie Lukin, Ashley Foots, Cassidy Henry, Matt Marge, Ron Artstein, David Traum, and Clare Voss. 2018. Human-robot dialogue and collaboration in search and navigation. In *LREC 2018 AREA Workshop (Annotation, Recognition and Evaluation of Actions)*.

Claire Bonial, Matthew Marge, Ron Artstein, Ashley Foots, Felix Gervits, Cory J. Hayes, Cassidy Henry, Susan G. Hill, Anton Leuski, Stephanie M. Lukin, Pooja Moolchandani, Kimberly A. Pollard, David R. Traum, and Clare R. Voss. 2017. Laying Down the Yellow Brick Road: Development of a Wizard-of-Oz Interface for Collecting Human-Robot Dialogue. In *AAAI Fall Symposium on Natural Communication for Human-Robot Collaboration*.

Bonnie Dorr and Doug Jones. 1996. Acquisition of Semantic Lexicons: Using Word Sense Disambiguation to Improve Precision. In *In Proceedings of the Workshop on Breadth and Depth of Semantic Lexicons, 34th Annual Conference of the Association for Computational Linguistics.* Kluwer Academic Publishers, pages 42–50.

Bonnie J. Dorr. 1993. *Machine Translation: A View from the Lexicon.* MIT Press, Cambridge, MA.

Bonnie J. Dorr. 1997. Large-Scale Dictionary Construction for Foreign Language Tutoring and Interlingual Machine Translation. *Machine Translation* 12:271–322.

Bonnie J. Dorr, Mari Olsen, Nizar Habash, and Scott Thomas. 2001. LCS Verb Database Documentation. http://www.umiacs.umd.edu/~bonnie/Demos/LCS_Database_Documentation.html.

Bonnie J. Dorr and Clare R. Voss. 1993. Machine Translation of Spatial Expressions: Defining the Relation between an Interlingua and a Knowledge Representation System . In *Proceedings of the Twelfth Conference of the American Association for Artificial Intelligence.* pages 374–379.

David Dowty. 1979. *Word Meaning and Montague Grammar.* Reidel, Dordrecht.

M. Guerssel, K. Hale, M. Laughren, B. Levin, and J. White Eagle. 1985. A Cross-linguistic Study of Transitivity Alternations. In W. H. Eilfort and P. D. Kroeber and K. L. Peterson, editor, *Papers from the Parasession in Causatives and Agentivity at the Twenty-first Regional meeting of the Chicago Linguistic Society.* pages 48–63.

Nizar Habash and Bonnie Dorr. 2003. A categorial variation database for english. In *In NAACL/HLT 2003, Proceedings of the Human Language Technology and North American Association for Computational Linguistics Conference.* pages 96–102.

Nizar Habash and Bonnie J. Dorr. 2002. Handling Translation Divergences: Combining Statistical and Symbolic Techniques in Generation-Heavy Machine Translation. In *Proceedings of the Fifth Conference of the Association for Machine Translation in the Americas.* Tiburon, CA, pages 84–93.

Nizar Habash, Bonnie J. Dorr, and Christof Monz. 2006. Challenges in Building an Arabic GHMT system with SMT Components. In *Proceedings of the 7th Conference of the Association for Machine Translation in the Americas.* Boston, MA, pages 56–65.

Jan Hajič, Eduard Bejček, Alevtina Bémová, Eva Buráňová, Eva Hajičová, Jiří Havelka, Petr Homola, Jiří Kárník, Václava Kettnerová, Natalia Klyueva, Veronika Kolářová, Lucie Kučová,

Markéta Lopatková, Marie Mikulová, Jiří Mírovsk, Anna Nedoluzhko, Petr Pajas, Jarmila Panevová, Lucie Poláková, Magdaléna Rysová, Petr Sgall, Johanka Spoustová, Pavel Straňák, Pavlína Synková, Magda evčíková, Jan tpánek, Zdeňka Ureová, Barbora Vidová Hladká, Daniel Zeman, Šárka Zikánová, and Zdeněk Žabokrtský. 2018. Prague dependency treebank 3.5. LINDAT/CLARIN digital library at the Institute of Formal and Applied Linguistics (ÚFAL), Faculty of Mathematics and Physics, Charles University. `http://hdl.handle.net/11234/1-2621`.

Ray Jackendoff. 1983. *Semantics and Cognition.* MIT Press, Cambridge, MA.

Ray Jackendoff. 1990. *Semantic Structures.* MIT Press, Cambridge, MA.

Ray Jackendoff. 1996. The Proper Treatment of Measuring Out, Telicity, and Perhaps Even Quantification in English. *Natural Language and Linguistic Theory* 14:305–354.

Karin Kipper, Anna Korhonen, Neville Ryant, and Martha Palmer. 2007. A Large-scale Classification of English Verbs. In *Language Resources and Evaluation.*

P. Kordjamshidi, M. Van Otterlo, and Marie-Francine Moens. 2010. Spatial Role Labeling: Task Definition and Annotation Scheme. In *Proceedings of Language Resources and Evaluation Conference.*

Raj Korpan, Susan L. Epstein, Anoop Aroor, and Gil Dekel. 2017. WHY: Natural Explanations from a Robot Navigator. In *AAAI 2017 Fall Symposium on Natural Communication for Human-Robot Collaboration.*

Geert-Jan Kruiff, Hendrik Zender, Patric Jensfelt, and Henrik Christensen. 2007. Situated dialogue and spatial organization: What, where ... and why? In *International Journal of Advanced Robotic Systems.*

Beth Levin. 1993. *English Verb Classes and Alternations: A Preliminary Investigation.* The University of Chicago Press.

Gina Levow, Bonnie J. Dorr, and Dekang Lin. 2000. Construction of Chinese-English Semantic Hierarchy for Cross-language Retrieval. In *ICCLC'2000 International Conference on Chinese Language Computing.*

Stephanie Lukin, Reginald Hobbs, and Clare Voss. 2018. A pipeline for creative visual storytelling. In *NAACL 2018 StoryNLP.*

M Marge, C Bonial, A Foots, C Hayes, C Henry, K Pollard, R Artstein, C Voss, and D Traum. 2017. Exploring Variation of Natural Human Commands to a Robot in a Collaborative Navigation Task. In *ACL2017 RoboNLP workshop.*

Nikolaos Mavridis and Deb Roy. 2006. Grounded situation models for robots: Where words and percepts meet. In *Proceedings of the IEEE/RSJ Conference on Intelligent Robots and Systems.*

Pooja Moolchandani, Cory Hayes, and Matthew Marge. 2018. Evaluating robot behavior in response to natural language. In *HRI '18 Companion: ACM/IEEE International Conference on Human-Robot Interaction Companion.*

Mari Broman Olsen, Bonnie J. Dorr, and Scott Thomas. 1997. Toward Compact Monotonically Compositional Interlingua Using Lexical Aspect. In *Proceedings of the Workshop on Interlinguas in MT.* San Diego, CA, pages 33–44.

Martha Palmer, Claire Bonial, and Jena D. Hwang. 2017. VerbNet: Capturing English Verb behavior, Meaning and Usage. In Susan Chipman, editor, *The Oxford Handbook of Cognitive Science*, Oxford University Press.

Katerina Pastra, Eirini Balta, Panagiotis Dimitrakis, and Giorgos Karakatsiotis. 2011. Embodied Language Processing: A New Generation of Language Technology. In *Language-Action Tools for Cognitive Artificial Agents: Papers from the 2011 AAAI Workshop (WS-11-14).*

Ian E. Perera, James F. Allen, Lucian Galescu, Choh Man Teng, Mark H. Burstein, Scott E. Friedman, David D. McDonald, and Jeffrey M. Rye. 2017. Natural Language Dialogue for Building and Learning Models and Structures. In *Proceedings of the Thirty-First AAAI Conference on Artificial Intelligence, February 4-9, 2017, San Francisco, California, USA..* pages 5103–5104.

J. Pustejovsky, J. L. Moszkowicz, and M. Verhagen. 2011. Using ISO-Space for Annotating Spatial Information. `http://www2.denizyuret.com/bib/pustejovsky/pustejovsky2011cosit/COSIT-ISO-Space.final.pdf`.

James Pustejovsky and Kiyong Lee. 2017. Enriching the Notion of Path in ISOspace. In *Proceedings of the 13th Joint ISO-ACL Workshop on Interoperable Semantic Annotation (ISA-13).*

Josef Ruppenhofer, Michael Ellsworth, Miriam R. L Petruck, Christopher R. Johnson, Collin F. Bakerand, and Jan Scheffczyk. 2016. Framenet ii: Extended theory and practice. `https://framenet.icsi.berkeley.edu/fndrupal/the_book`.

Michael Spranger, Jakob Suchan, and Mehul Bhatt. 2016. Robust Natural Language Processing Combining Reasoning, Cognitive Semantics, and Construction Grammar for Spatial Language. In *Proceedings of the Twenty-Fifth International Joint Conference on Artificial Intelligence.*

Amber Stubbs and James Pustejovsky. 2012. *Natural Language Annotation for Machine Learning*. O'Reilly Media.

Leonard Talmy. 2014. Foreward: Past, present, and future of motion research. In Iraide Ibarretxe-Antugano, editor, *Motion and Space across Languages: Theory and Applications. HCP (Human Cognitive Processing) Series*, John Benjamins.

Thora Tenbrink. 2011. Reference frames of space and time in language. In *Journal of Pragmatics*. volume 43, pages 704–722.

D Traum, C Henry, S Lukin, R Artstein, F Gervitz, K Pollard, C Bonial, S Lei, C Voss, M Marge, C Hayes, and S Hill. 2018. Dialogue Structure Annotation for Multi-Floor Interaction. In *LREC*.

David Traum and Nizar Habash. 2000. Generation from Lexical Conceptual Structures. In *Proceedings of the Workshop on Applied Interlinguas, North American Association for Computational Linguistics / Applied NLP Conference*. pages 34–41.

Lucy Vanderwende, Arul Menezes, and Chris Quirk. 2015. An amr parser for english, french, german, spanish and japanese and a new amr-annotated corpus. In *HLT-NAACL*.

Clare Voss and Bonnie J. Dorr. 1995. Toward a Lexicalized Grammar for Interlinguas. *J. of Machine Translation* 10:14–3.

Clare R. Voss, Bonnie J. Dorr, and M. U. Şencan. 1998. Lexical Allocation in Interlingua-based Machine Translation of Spatial Expressions. In Patrick Oliver and Klaus-Peter Gapp, editors, *Representation and Processing of Spatial Expressions*, L. Erlbaum Associates Inc., Hillsdale, NJ, USA, pages 133–148.

Author Index

Association for Computational Linguistics
209 N. Eighth Street
Stroudsburg, Pennsylvania 18360

ISBN 978-1-5108-6363-7